Give yourself a
RAISE

"I have read hundreds of books on personal finance over the years, most leaving me with questions and a few answers. *Give Yourself a RAISE* breaks that tradition and gives regular people and families, [who] work hard for what they have, practical and useful advice to help them bring more order to their personal finances. My family just managed **a $12,000 raise** by following Gordon Bennett Bleil's advice."

—DOUGLAS COOK, CPA, MBA, CIC

"Gordon's book was an informational and motivational one. He outlines concepts in a way that makes sense to me. I feel more in control of my finances and my future: His book changed my life!"

—SUZANNE DARROW, *Director of Distance Learning for a major healthcare organization*

"Every time I have had him [Bleil] conduct classes whether for beginners or seasoned senior bankers, the reviews have been outstanding. . . . In my opinion, there is simply none better. . . .

"I would be remiss if I did not recognize his new book on personal money management, *Give Yourself a RAISE*. . . . It is a really practical guide for anyone struggling to gain control of their finances. I have been so impressed that I have recommended this be used as part of the curriculum of our church's money management class."

—THOMAS T. HAWKER, *Commercial banker for 40 years and most recently retired President and CEO of a publicly traded regional bank and holding company in California*

SECOND EDITION

Give yourself a
RAISE

how to have

- ☑ **more money**
- ☑ **less stress**
- ☑ **financial freedom**

GORDON BENNETT BLEIL

ELATE PRESS
LEDERACH, PENNSYLVANIA

Published in 2013 by Elate Press
P.O. Box 238
Lederach, PA 19450-0238
www.ptff.net

First Edition, 2010
Second Edition, 2013

Publisher's Cataloging-in-Publication Data
(Prepared by The Donohue Group, Inc.)
Bleil, Gordon Bennett, 1932-
  Give yourself a raise : how to have more money, less stress, financial freedom / Gordon Bennett Bleil. -- 2nd ed.
    p. ; cm.
  First edition published in 2010 with author's name as Gordon Bennett.
  Issued also as an ebook.
  Includes bibliographical references.
  ISBN: 978-0-9886149-1-8
  1. Finance, Personal. 2. Financial risk. 3. Debt. I. Title.
HG179 .B54 2013
332.024

Printed in the United States of America
10 9 8 7 6 5 4 3 2 1

Digital Edition: ISBN 978-0-9886149-2-5

Editing by Deborah Lynes and Patty Hodgins, D&D Editorial Services
Book design by Fiona Raven and Linda Parke, www.fionaraven.com

The paper used in this publication meets the minimum requirements of the American National Standard for Information Sciences—Permanence of Paper for Printed Library Materials, ANSI Z39.48-1992.

To

Pat, for encouraging me

Debbie, for her insights

Contents

Preface to the Second Edition

"Why still another book on personal money management?" you may ask. Because in spite of the wide array of advice books on money, finance, investing, and debt management, tens of thousands of people are still really stressed about their money situations. The money crisis in our society is monumental. Whatever books are out there, the problems still exist.

This book is simple enough and practical enough that you can at last take charge of the money in your life. The benefit is getting rid of the stress and conflict that being out of control with your money puts into your daily life.

I wrote the core of this book over twenty years ago for a community bank client that wanted to give its customers a class in money management. At that time very few people were maxed out on multiple credit cards, home mortgages required 20 percent down payment, home equity loans or lines of credit were unknown, and job stability was taken for granted.

Today's economic environment is frighteningly different. Real estate lending of over 100 percent value has fueled irrational spending and blind faith that the future will take care of itself. Until the last few years, everyone assumed the value of houses would simply continue to go up. Credit cards proliferated and provided an easy way to get deeply in debt. People hocked their future expected income streams for "have it now" spending. In the fall of 2008, in the midst of this "easy credit" environment, the U.S. economy entered a credit crisis that appeared to be spiraling into a period of severe recession. As a result, many people lost their jobs unexpectedly.

The consequences are serious and negative. People are facing foreclosure and/or bankruptcy. Couples are squabbling about money. Conflict over money is the leading cause of divorce. And, of course, money worries cause stress that affects health, work performance, and personal relationships.

Merle Travis's song "16 Tons," a hit in 1947, seems just as true today:

You load 16 tons, what do you get?
Another day older and deeper in debt.
St. Peter don't you call me 'cause I can't go.
I owe my soul to the company store.

Simply substitute "Visa," "MasterCard," or some other lender for "company store" and you have today's situation. Debt bondage is not good for you.

A slowing economy does not necessarily lead to personal disaster unless it is paired with some other circumstances. The person or family that has been consistently living within their means, has little or no debt, and has an emergency reserve of a few months' income has choices for getting through tough times. But when almost every dollar of income is already committed to pay for yesterday's decisions, even a small blip in income or expenses triggers a crisis. Is this where you are?

Prerequisites

To determine whether you are ready for this book, read the next six paragraphs:

1. Are you miserable or maybe even desperate about your financial situation? You will never get out of your misery or despair about money until you hurt so badly that you finally want to change. Anything less than this and you will simply try to wait things out until they somehow magically get better. Things do not get better by ignoring them, so you are still going to be in trouble. Insanity has been defined as doing the same thing repeatedly and expecting different results, or "if you always do what you have always done, you will always get what you have always gotten." Until you hurt badly enough from your bad habits, you will not have the drive and focus to change them.

2. You have to admit that what you have been doing is not working and that what is needed is not a quick fix but a permanent change in how you handle money.

3. You have to believe that you can be successful with the program. If you start out thinking your situation is hopeless, it is. Get over the

negative and have faith that you will accomplish what you set out to do. As the saying goes, "If you think you can or if you think you can't, you are probably right." Do not bet against yourself.

4. You must accept the concept of being *totally and permanently out of debt*. Debt is like a prison: It takes away your choices.

5. You must be willing to commit seriously to making permanent significant change. If you are out of shape physically and buy a treadmill for exercise, you know you have to get on it and use it for you to get any benefit. Getting in "fiscal shape" requires the same focus and long-term perspective as getting in physical shape.

6. You must be realistic about how long this will take. This is not a one-week program or even a one-year program—it is a life style and a lifetime change. Your initial planning and setup will take several hours over a one- or two-week period, and then you will be managing your money one step at a time. After the program is set up, you can manage it with about an hour a month.

What This Book Is Not

Investment strategy and technique books are plentiful, and I recommend you read as many of them as you can. However, until you have money to invest, they are premature. If you are running out of money every month before the month is over, you need to get a grip on your money life. This book is not another budget system or budget plan. Budgets work for some people, but the vast majority of people soon abandon a budget because of the required daily rigid control and upkeep. Most budgets are too detailed and inflexible. Yes, I do use the term *budget* and explain it in some detail in Chapter 2. However, I prefer to think in terms of a "spending plan" rather than a "budget," which conjures up images of penny-by-penny tracking.

I do not present a magic formula or never-before-revealed secret in this book. Magic is an illusion behind which there is always an explanation, no matter how well concealed. No magic except the results of consistently applying the plan will be revealed.

Summary

Once when trying to strip off some extra pounds, I spotted a book on how to lose weight through yoga. It was a very thick book. I knew that every book has a pearl of wisdom buried somewhere between its covers. With some browsing I discovered the yoga pearl: "FAST!" The rest of the book was how to have a positive mental attitude while starving to death.

The pearls of wisdom embedded in *Give Yourself a RAISE* were summarized long ago in the classic by George S. Clason, *The Richest Man in Babylon*: Pay yourself first and live within your means.

Start now to make those simple truths work for you. This book shows you how to do it.

Reflections on the Initial Edition of This Book

Since releasing the first edition of this book, I have learned how important the lessons I try to teach are in the lives of many individuals. Statistics tell us that over 50 percent of American families have issues with financial matters and that financial issues remain among the leading causes of divorce in this country. The stress caused by financial issues is incalculable and affects everything from our work performance to our health.

For me, forming good financial habits is the goal of this book, and from first-hand experience, I know that what I have written can help a huge number of people. If you have any comments or suggestions how this work can be made better, I would welcome hearing from you. Economic times are very tough for a large number of people and anything we can do to help ease the burden is worthwhile.

Acknowledgments

Maybe there are authors who can write a book "solo," without help, encouragement, and critique from others. I do not know them.

For me, this has been a collaborative process among three key support players each of whom invaluably enriched the final result. Without their constant nudging, it is unlikely that the project would have ever been finished. My wife, my editor, and my designer all filled critical roles just when they were needed.

Pat, my wife, is and has been the inspiration for whatever I have embarked upon. She provides the day-in-day-out positive aura essential for motivation. Beyond that, she is a scholar in her own right and has contributed significantly to the end product.

My editor, Deborah Lynes, was ideal for her role. In one of my earlier lives I owned a small publishing company and was well aware of the need for professional expertise. As I began pulling together diverse notes assembled over many years, Deborah came on board as the project's manager and developmental editor. It has been a wonderful relationship, and as anyone who has ever written knows, a skilled editor is essential. The flow and structure simply would not have happened without her guidance.

Words and ink and paper are not enough. Without design they remain only raw materials. Fiona Raven is a designer with a rare combination of artistic talent, training, and experience coupled with a compulsive attention to detail. She is good (very good), responsive, and fun to work with.

My deepest thanks to all of you for your caring and guidance. And, of course, the final responsibility is mine should anyone find this work wanting.

Introduction

The Leaking Bucket

If you pour water into a bucket with holes, you absolutely know that all of the water will leak out. The water may leak out slowly if the holes are few and small, or it may leak out very quickly if the holes are many and large. But it will all leak out.

So it is with money. Money is like the water in a bucket. If your spending bucket is full of holes, some of your money simply leaks out without giving you any pleasure at all. In fact, chances are that a lot of money is leaking out and you are not even aware of it. Plug the holes in your money bucket and you will be giving yourself a "raise."

You will be amazed at how simple it is to structure your money habits and plug all of the leaks that are now depriving you of the full enjoyment of the money you work so hard to earn. This book will show you an incredibly simple and powerful way to take charge of your money and get rid of financial stress in your life. At the end of this chapter is a list of symptoms of a leaking bucket. If only one of the items pertains to you, this book will benefit you.

About This Book

This book is really two books. Part 1, particularly the first eight chapters, provides a how-to-do-it approach for taking control of your financial life. It focuses on the steps you need to take and the system you need to put in place to eliminate financial waste (plugging the holes in the bucket), get rid of stress caused by money issues, and put your financial life on a positive path.

In Chapter 1 you will start with a quick and insightful assessment of your own Financial Freedom Risk, based on some key factors. This risk assessment quiz will pinpoint exactly what needs to change in your financial life. After a brief introduction to why objectives and plans are important, you will gather a history of where your money has been going. Chapter 4 teaches you how to set specific goals and match them to your historical spending patterns. It is the foundation for setting up a truly powerful and simple money management system, the core of Chapter 6.

That system, the Freedom Money Management System,™ is a powerful program that uses the sophistication of electronic banking to simplify staying in control of your finances forever.

Part 2 is a series of short essays, or primers, on a variety of topics that impact your financial existence. Each of these topics deserves to be an entire book itself, and in fact many easy-to-access books and reference materials do exist for each topic. I include the essays in Part 2 to familiarize you with some of the critical issues that impact your financial life and to motivate you to continue your financial literacy education.

Meet Your New Best Friend—the Invisible Electronic Banker

If you are not using the vast array of services (most of which are free) offered by your personal banker, you are missing out on some of the most powerful tools of personal money management. Just a few years ago, it was inconceivable that such systems would be practical for managing your day-to-day finances. Now it is foolish not to take advantage of these services, and the Freedom Money Management System™ described in Part 1 of this book will show you how.

The full benefit of the bank's services is obtained when you conduct your banking business on-line with your home computer. On-line banking eliminates almost all need to ever personally visit a physical bank location. However, even if you do not use a computer, you can still take advantage of the electronic revolution by working with your bank to structure your accounts to simplify and automate much of your money management activity.

If your paycheck, retirement check, or Social Security benefit is being automatically deposited into a bank account, you are already using electronic banking in its simplest form. The next step is to use the bank to route the money into savings and to pay your bills.

Some of the advantages of electronic banking are:

- You rarely have to visit a bank personally.

- You can do your banking 24/7: 24 hours a day, 7 days a week, whenever it is most convenient for you.

- An instant up-to-the-minute balance is always available.

- On-line banking is perfectly safe and secure.

- Electronic banking is very simple to learn.

- No postage is required.

- A payment can be entered the day a bill arrives to be paid on the date the bill is due so you have the use of the most of your money for the longest time.

- A record of all payments to every vendor or payee is instantly available.

- Late payments are a thing of the past. Payments won't be in the mail to go astray.

- Transfers among accounts are very simple.

- Multiple accounts can be easily managed.

- Electronic banking takes less time than writing checks.

- Many paper bills can be eliminated—you can receive electronic bills instead. An e-bill minimizes your risk of identity theft from Dumpster divers or mailbox thieves.

- Personal discipline is developed while using these simple systems.

- Accounts are very flexible and can change easily as your needs change.

This book will teach you how to use bank accounts to take control of your personal money management.

The Fundamentals of Money Management

The fundamentals of successful money management found in this book and espoused by every financial consultant are very simple and proven to work:

Rule 1: Pay yourself first.

Rule 2: Live within your means.

Rule 3: Stay out of debt.

These are the rules. Implementing them is what this book is about. Depending on your present circumstances, it may be easy or hard to follow the rules, but the steps in this book can be followed by anyone and are lifelong plans. Once you have a plan in place, it can be adjusted to your changing needs.

A comprehensive money management plan builds on four basic components, somewhat like the legs of a table:

1. Setting objectives and goals.

2. Creating a spending plan.

3. Managing debt.

4. Accumulating savings.

Goal setting comes first because without goals, setting priorities for how and when you will spend your money makes no sense.

Why You Need This Book

No matter where you are in life today, the odds are that the future has some changes in store for you. These changes may be positive or negative but will likely be a mix of both. Money is a common denominator in everyone's life, so a properly functioning money management system is essential for dealing with changes in your life. A poor system will make negative changes worse and may hinder taking advantage of positive changes. In short, a good money management system is fundamental to a stress-free everyday life.

If you are just starting out on your career path, your life is pretty simple: One wage earner, one spender who is accountable to no one. For you the challenge is to stay debt free and develop healthy money habits that will serve you in the future.

Later you may take on more obligations, like buying a house. Life becomes more complicated when you become a homeowner. Maintenance costs can catch you unaware, property taxes come as a surprise right after you spend a bundle on a fancy vacation, and you have to become a better steward of your resources. Again, the challenge is to stay debt free.

When you enter into a sharing relationship with someone else, it is imperative that you have a sound money management system. Now there may be two wage earners and two (or more) spenders. For married couples, money is the leading cause of conflict and ultimately divorce.

And let's not ignore families headed by a single parent. These families present endless complicated money-juggling challenges. The system outlined in this book is ideal for those situations, too.

Your system of spending must account for different styles and different priorities and leave each party comfortable with the fairness of the system.

The Freedom Money Management System™ detailed in Chapter 6 accommodates all of these differences and changes. It is the only system you will need throughout your life. It changes easily as your needs change.

If you are just starting out, the system will help you avoid common mistakes. If you are in a later phase and already have high stress in your financial life, the system will give you a way to reduce that stress. If you are deep in debt and struggling to make ends meet, the system will guide you back to sound management of your money.

One Size Does Not Fit All

The *concepts* set forth in this book are fundamental and will serve anyone. What differs from person to person is the required amount of detail and control.

A single wage earner/single spender may have little need for elaborate record keeping and tracking of expenses. When there are multiple wage earners, multiple spenders, and lots of significant expenses, more control is essential.

The Freedom Money Management System™ expands to meet more complex situations. The system grows as needed without starting over.

Problems with Traditional Budgets

A rigid budget that attempts to predict every dollar of spending and that requires extensive record keeping will be abandoned in short order. You may have experienced using such budgets yourself. There is no way to anticipate the future to the level of detail required to make these systems work.

Comfort drives everything. We all go to great lengths to avoid discomfort. A simple plan with which you are comfortable that you follow is superior to an elaborate plan that is uncomfortable and that you consequently ignore. The plan is not the focus; achieving the plan is the focus.

The Freedom Money Management System™ is as simple as it gets. Within broad guidelines, the plan allows users discretion to spend money any way they want and still keep the system intact.

Financial Literacy

Literacy is defined as "being knowledgeable." The scope of money-related areas in our lives is vast. You should learn about each of these areas so you can both take advantage of the benefits they offer and avoid the risks they pose. Part 2 of this book (Chapters 10 through 17) will introduce you to the following key money-related topics that affect your life.

Preparing for Your Future

As you gain control of your current finances, you need to begin to look to the future. If you expect to stop working someday, you simply must set aside enough money to replace your paycheck. Part 2 covers the basics of investment options and retirement (Chapter 10), an understanding of risk (Chapter 11), and an awareness of how government programs can help you meet your goals (Chapter 12) to give you a starting point.

Protecting What You Have

Once you have money, you certainly don't want to lose it. Insurance (Chapter 13) is one tool to protect what you have, but you need to have the right insurance. The price of insurance is an important consideration because you have to have enough insurance but do not want to spend more than is necessary or have too much insurance.

Unfortunately, there are always those among us who would rather steal than work and that means you are a potential target of crime (Chapter 14).

Not long ago, most commonly we feared losing our valuables through personal physical attack. Now, because we live in an electronic era, criminals can steal from us electronically before we even know it. Chapter 14 gives a quick introduction to credit scores and identity theft and directions for self-protection.

Finally, you need a comprehensive emergency plan, and Chapter 15 reviews the basics for you to get started.

Making More Money

"Why," you may ask, "are some people making so much more money than I am?" "Is there a way for me to join the ranks of the better paid?" The answer is: Maybe.

Chapter 16 covers two key factors that explain why anyone is making a lot of money. Chapter 17 details five rules for success that will help you chart a course to land more highly paid jobs.

Because you will have implemented the solid money management system we cover in Part 1, you will keep what you earn. The leaking bucket will be a thing of the past.

Do These Symptoms of a Leaking Bucket Describe You?

You have a leaking bucket (and you have the potential to give yourself a raise) if any of the following describes you:

- You are in debt and the amount you owe is growing.

- You are making late payments.

- You are bouncing checks.

- Your credit score is low.

- You are not taking care of personal health matters because you are broke.

- You are paying only the minimum each month on your credit cards.

- You are facing increasing mortgage payments as a variable-rate loan rate increases.

- You do not have six months' emergency living expenses in near-cash investments.

- Your personal relationships are stressed because of money issues.

- You worry a lot about tomorrow.

- You cannot afford the vacation you want to take.

- Your job is not secure.

- You do not have a realistic retirement plan.

- You are unhappy with the way you are managing money now.

The longer you wait to deal with these issues, the worse the problems will become.

A Financial Health Assessment

To plug the leaks in your bucket and give yourself a raise, you need to understand your own situation. This assessment will require some effort on your part, but after all, it took some effort to get into your financial "pickle," so you should expect to make some effort to get out of it.

First, spend a few minutes taking the simple Financial Freedom Risk Assessment quiz in Chapter 1 and calculate your Final Risk Score (this quiz is also available on our Web site, www.ptff.net)—this test is a quick *snapshot of where you are.* If your Final Risk Score is low, you need help NOW and this book can help you. However, even if you have a high risk score, you can benefit from this book if any of the preceding "leaking bucket" statements describes your situation.

Next, you need to assemble data on your own financial history to understand *where you have been over the past year.* This data will allow you to detect potential leaks in your financial bucket and identify where you have the potential for plugging the leaks and giving yourself a raise.

Summary

Money management is, as the cliché says, "not rocket science." The payoff for a modest amount of effort and planning is enormous. Take the challenge a step at a time and you will be amazed at how skillful you become in a short period.

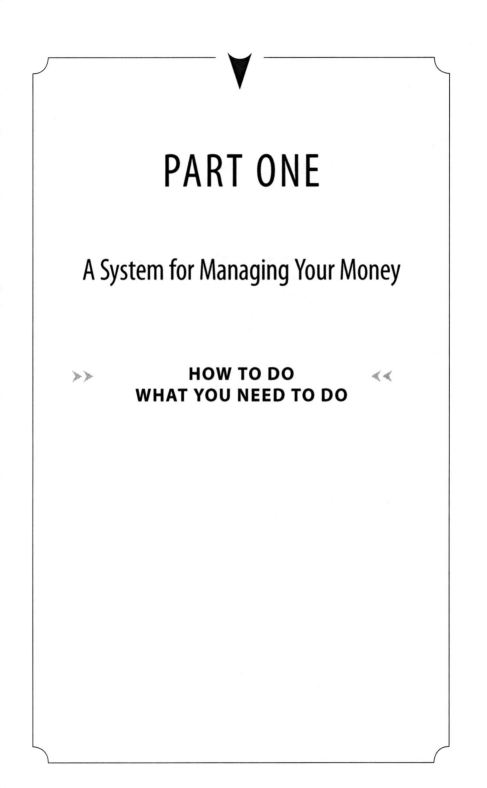

PART ONE

A System for Managing Your Money

**HOW TO DO
WHAT YOU NEED TO DO**

Overview

This is a beginner's book about the fundamentals of taking care of your own finances. Based on the number of bankruptcies and home foreclosures and amount of credit card debt, there are a whole lot of people who apparently never had the basics presented to them. Or they ignored them.

If you are struggling with the "how-to-do-it" problems of day-to-day money management and the stress and conflict of being out of control, the basics in this book will provide direction for a lifetime. It isn't complicated. It isn't hard. But it takes a commitment to be in control of your finances.

Once you have a money management system in place, you can then benefit from the wisdom of literally hundreds of authors on how to magnify your wealth. But as long as you are running out of money before you reach your next pay period, or if you are addicted to borrowing to make up for the shortfall, you need to master the basics.

Part 1 presents just enough philosophy on why you need to do what you need to do to understand the underlying practicality of the system I recommend. It then gives you a step-by-step process, sample forms, and plenty of flexibility to create your own system.

The section starts with an assessment of your financial health; then leads you through creating a financial plan (and the reasons that is important) by looking at your past history and forecasting the changes you want (or need) to make; and concludes by showing you the twenty-first-century way to use electronic banking and a plan to eliminate the debt "hangover."

Welcome to controlling your finances.

CHAPTER ONE

The Financial Freedom Risk Assessment Quiz

Before you can figure out how to give yourself a raise, you need to determine how financially "sick" you are (how leaky your financial bucket is and where the leaks are).

When you are physically sick enough to seek medical advice, the doctor first wants to know your symptoms. Where do you hurt? Next, the doctor gathers your vital signs (weight, temperature, pulse, and blood pressure) to help make an early diagnosis and point you on a path to recovery. The doctor will also want to know what has changed and what trends you have observed. Are you getting better or worse? This initial consultation may be followed by more elaborate tests, all of which are designed to give the doctor the information necessary to prescribe a way back to feeling better.

If you are reading this book, the odds are that you are "fiscally" sick. Your money health is bad enough for you to seek professional help. But how sick are you? What are the key numbers that can point you to a prescription for restoring and maintaining your fiscal health? What are your fiscal vital signs?

Take the following Financial Freedom Risk Assessment quiz. It will take 5 to 10 minutes. The Final Risk Score that you calculate will give you a quick snapshot of the extent to which your financial freedom is at risk. A doctor does not treat you for being well; the doctor focuses on what is wrong or out of balance. This quiz pinpoints what you need to do to get financially "well." And even better, it will let you see the areas where you are already well so you can concentrate specifically on what deserves your attention.

If your Final Risk Score is high, you may want to skip ahead in the book. But before you skip ahead, remember that *staying* well when you are in good health is as important as *getting* well when you are sick. The quiz questions provide a guideline for what fiscal wellness looks like. Let's move on to the quiz and your own personal diagnosis.

The Financial Freedom Risk Assessment Quiz

What is financial freedom and just how risky is your present situation? And if your financial freedom is at risk, what steps can you take to reduce that risk? The discussion below will help you answer these critical financial questions.

Simply put, financial freedom is the ability you have to make choices every day about how you will spend your money. Money in your pocket offers an infinite number of opportunities for spending it. But once you have purchased something with your pocket money, you have exchanged freedom of choice for the item you bought. Another way to think of it: You can only spend a dollar once. When it's gone, it's gone.

Spending money you do not have by borrowing to buy something now (buying "on credit") immediately reduces your future financial freedom. You have given up your future choices about how to spend future income. Debt directly reduces your financial freedom.

The following key factors provide the basis for assessing your Financial Freedom Risk. After the description of each factor is a list of statements with a point value for each. Select the one statement that best describes your present situation and circle the number. When you have finished all the factors, add up the circled numbers plus your points from Factor 10. The total is your Final Risk Score.

Factor 1: How Stable Is Your Job or Source of Income?

Income from wages or investments determines what you have available to pay your bills and maintain your life style. Many have been surprised recently to discover that jobs can be eliminated rapidly and that investment values can plummet. Nothing is more important than a realistic analysis of how safe your entire income is. Even a seemingly small reduction in your income may have the potential to become a crisis. Also, do not overlook the real possibility that a health issue or an accident can interrupt your income.

Review the following statements, select the one that best describes your present situation, and circle the number.

0   You are unemployed and have no regular income.

2   You work part-time or seasonally or your income is unpredictable.

4   You are in a situation that has a high probability of layoffs.

6   You have a job but you are not sure it will last.

8   You have only a very small chance of losing your job.

10   Your job is stable or you have a reliable source of income.

Factor 2: Do You Have an Emergency Cash Fund?

If your income stops or is suddenly reduced, how will you pay your bills? Some expenses are entirely discretionary and can be stopped immediately. Others can be postponed for a while, but the bulk of your expenses cannot be eliminated or scaled back quickly. To minimize your risk, you need an emergency cash fund to tide you over. The more, the better.

Review the following statements, select the one that best describes your present situation, and circle the number.

0   You have no cash, no credit.

2   Unexpected expenses will be put on a credit card or postponed.

4   Enough money is set aside for only one month's expenses.

6   More than one month's but less than six months' expenses are available.

8   You have over six months' but less than one year's expenses available.

10   Greater than one year's total expenses are readily available.

Factor 3: Do You Have Goals?

A story is told about Professor Albert Einstein that occurred on the train one morning. It seems that he had gotten on board but could not locate his ticket. The conductor assured him that he was well known and they were not worried about his ticket and that he had paid his fare. About half an hour later, they saw the professor frantically looking for his ticket. The conductor again assured him, "We know who you are professor so don't worry about it." He replied, "I know who I am, but I have no idea where I'm going."

So it is with goals. If you do not know where you are going, any place will get you there. And, what you will learn about goals applies to all of your life, not just your finances. Goals will get you started on the right path.

Review the following statements, select the one that best describes your present situation, and circle the number.

0   You have no goals. Life is just day to day.

2   You have only a faint idea of where you want to end up.

4   You have an approximate one-year to five-year plan.

6   Your goals are broken down into some specific categories and time frames.

8   Your goals are very specific for a long time frame but are not written down.

10   You have written goals.

Factor 4: What Is Your Debt Level (not including home mortgage)?

Nothing robs you of financial freedom faster than debt. Since most people need a mortgage to buy a home and most find it necessary to finance an automobile, the analysis in this book focuses on short-term debt—the credit card kind—that suggests you are living beyond your means. If your income is interrupted or reduced, the best situation is to have the fewest number of bills that must be paid. More debt means fewer choices.

Review the following statements, select the one that best describes your present situation, and circle the number.

0   You are deeply in debt. Bankruptcy is a possibility.

2   Debt is *increasing* and is over six months' income.

4   Debt is *increasing* and is between one to six months' income.

5   Debt is *decreasing* but is over six months' income.

6   Debt is *decreasing* and is between one and six months' income.

8   Debt not being paid off monthly is less than one month's income.

10   Balances are paid off monthly and you have no current debt.

Factor 5: What Is the Estimated Value of Your House?

The less money you owe as a percent of the value of your home, the better off you are. Even in periods of sharply declining real estate values, your home should be a stabilizing factor in your life. Here is how to calculate the loan-to-value (LTV) percentage for your house. Divide the outstanding *principal* balance of your mortgage by the market value of your house. Example: Outstanding principal mortgage balance, $250,000. House market value, $325,000. $250,000/$325,000 = 77 percent.

Review the following statements, select the one that best describes your present situation, and circle the number.

0   You are behind in payments and foreclosure is a real possibility.

2   Your home is worth less than you paid for it.

4   Your home is worth about what you paid for it.

6   You have up to 50 percent equity in your home.

8   You have over 50 percent equity in your home.

10   You have no mortgage (house is debt free or you rent).

Factor 6: How Much Do You Spend on Housing Including Your Mortgage?

The more of your income that goes toward housing, the fewer choices you have in a period of reduced income. Like debt, housing costs are difficult to reduce in the short term. These costs include your mortgage payment (or rent), home equity loans, property taxes, insurance, and utility bills.

Review the following statements, select the one that best describes your present situation, and circle the number.

0   Your housing costs are greater than 60 percent of gross income.

2   Housing costs are between 50 and 59 percent of gross income.

4   Housing costs are between 38 and 49 percent of gross income.

6   Housing costs are between 30 and 37 percent of gross income.

10   Housing costs are less than 30 percent of gross income.

Factor 7: How Much Are Your Mandatory Living Expenses (bills you have to pay)?

When disaster or the unexpected setback comes calling, you are going to want to start cutting back on everything you can. The first thing, of course, is discretionary spending. But there is always a point beyond which you cannot cut and that is mandatory spending. If the amount is huge, what amounts to a mere inconvenience may turn into a crisis. So your objective is to keep the mandatory expenses portion of your budget as low as possible so you will be better able to deal with adverse circumstances.

Review the following statements, select the one that best describes your present situation, and circle the number.

0   You live month to month and have nothing left over.

2   Mandatory expenses are over 90 percent of your gross income.

4   Mandatory expenses are over 75 percent of your gross income.

6   Mandatory expenses are over 50 percent of your gross income.

8   Mandatory expenses are over 35 percent of your gross income.

10   Mandatory expenses are less than 35 percent of your gross income.

Factor 8: How Are You Protecting Your Assets?

At one of the fires in the hills of California several years ago, a fireman and a former homeowner were looking at the remains of a home that had burned to the ground. "I assume," said the fireman, "that you had insurance on the house?" "No," replied the homeowner, "I did not." "Why?" asked the fireman. "Because I never needed it before!" said the homeowner.

As you accumulate assets in life, you must take whatever steps are necessary to protect those assets, unless, of course, you can afford to lose them. Anything that you cannot afford to lose or do not want to give up—including your ability to earn a living—must be protected.

Review the following statements, select the one that best describes your present situation, and circle the number.

0   You do not have any insurance.

2   You have insurance only on your car.

4   You have home owners' (or renters') insurance and automobile insurance.

6   You have all of the above and enough life and health insurance.

8   You have all of the above plus a personal umbrella policy.

10   You have all of the above plus long-term-care insurance if you are over 55.

Factor 9: How Are You Preparing for Retirement?

Only you will look out for you. You need time on your side to accumulate enough money and assets during your working years to replace your wages when you stop working (when you retire).

Review the following statements, select the one that best describes your present situation, and circle the number.

0   You have no plan and make no current contributions toward retirement.

2   You make only occasional contributions to a retirement plan.

4   Up to 9 percent of gross income regularly being set aside for retirement.

6   10 percent of gross income being set aside for retirement.

8   More than 10 percent of gross income routinely being set aside for retirement.

10   Enough is being set aside to meet all of your goals.

Factor 10: Bonus Questions

Of course, many more items have an impact on your financial freedom. The following short list of a few more items that experts say have an impact on your financial freedom will give you some additional insights. Most writers on financial management agree that each of the following is an important part of a healthy financial life.

Review the items below and give yourself one point for each item that applies to you.

_____ You have a will or a living trust.

_____ You have powers of attorney.

_____ You have health care emergency arrangements.

_____ You review your credit report three times a year.

_____ Your family is fully informed of all of your financial plans.

_____ You have an accurate accessible inventory of all your important papers.

_____ You have a fee-only professional advisor with whom you meet at least annually.

_____ Your computer files are backed up regularly.

_____ Your debit card is not linked to any of your major assets.

_____ You read and study financial matters regularly.

Evaluation of Your Financial Health

Now add up all of your individual scores. The total is your Final Risk Score. This score is a quick look at your present financial freedom. Where does your score fall on the following spectrum?

Final Risk Score (a higher score indicates less risk to financial freedom)

90 – 100	Amazing. You are doing nearly everything right.
80 – 89	Excellent. Pay attention to any risk factor with a score less than 6.

70 – 79	Good. Make changes now where the risk score is 4 or less.
60 – 69	Fair. Any deterioration is dangerous. Find things to change.
50 – 59	Poor. Serious trouble is lurking if anything gets worse.
Below 50	Disaster? Your challenge is enormous and urgent.

If you are living beyond your means or are deeply in debt, your Final Risk Score will pinpoint immediately what you need to change. It is time for some serious goal setting and planning for the future.

What Do You Want to Do Now?

After taking the quiz, how do you feel about your financial health (or lack of it)? Are you comfortable with your risk level? But more important, if you are unhappy with your present situation, are you really ready to do something about it? Unless you are completely committed to having a different financial future, neither this book nor any other will help you. There are no shortcuts to taking charge of your life.

The simple truth is that repeating the behavior or habits that got you where you are today will not change things. You have to have a clear focus and the resolve to do whatever it takes to change your financial life.

It is simple to describe what needs to be done, but it is never easy to do it. Habits are hard to change.

Look over the questions on which you had the lowest (most damning) points. What can you do to change those scores? What will have the fastest impact and reduce your financial freedom risk the most without at the same time making another score worse?

There are three steps in the process of improving your financial risk:

1. Stop things from getting worse. Stabilize your situation.

2. Restore your financial health with a systematic program to make things better—to be where you want to be.

3. Maintain your financial health and prevent your financial situation from deteriorating in the future.

How Long Will It Take?

The lower your risk score, the longer it will take to change your life.

Small changes may be enough to stop a bad *trend*. If you are essentially living within your means but slip into self-indulgence and run up some small amount of credit card debt, you may be able to fix things in a few months. If you stop buying on credit and cut out some discretionary expenses like lattes, movies, and restaurants, it may be enough to get you on a long-term healthy track quickly.

However, if you have been subsidizing your life style with debt, have been borrowing for quite a while, and are facing some income reversals, it is going to take longer to adjust your habits, pay off your debts, and get on a pay-as-you-go basis. A year or two is not unreasonable.

The worst case is one in which your realistic income and your life style expenses are completely out of balance. You may have to seriously consider strategies such as selling your house and moving to a smaller one, selling a car or getting a less expensive one, and other major changes. This could take years.

What Is Next?

Until you have a realistic picture of where your money is going now, you cannot begin to make the changes that will plug the holes in your leaking money bucket and head you toward a fiscal wellness plan. Chapter 3 focuses on gathering that spending history.

Giving yourself a raise is a three-pronged process. First—and the easiest way to get more money—is to find the leaks in your money bucket (by looking at your spending history) and plug them up. Second, once the leaks are plugged, modify your spending habits to match your income. And third, explore ways to actually increase your income.

Oh, by the Way

If a grim financial picture is not enough to motivate you to change, consider your physical health. Stress is bad, really bad. And nobody disputes that money issues are a leading cause of personal stress. We know that money issues are a leading cause of marital discord and divorce.

The choice is yours. Surely you can take charge of your money life.

≫≫   *The Health Risks of Stress*   ≪≪

Dr. J. Doyle Walton, Cardiologist

As an interventional cardiologist, I treat people having life-threatening heart attacks on a regular basis. Acutely interrupting a potentially lethal event is both dramatic and satisfying. Despite this, the real "action" is in prevention, and this is the cornerstone of all strategies to maintain optimal health.

"Stress" is a somewhat nebulous concept, as it is difficult to measure and means different things to different people. We all feel it, live with it, and do our best to manage it on a daily basis. Despite this, stress frequently manifests in illness and trips to the doctor or hospital. The association of common stress-related ailments such as depression and anxiety with poor health outcomes is well known to physicians and supported by an ever-growing body of peer-reviewed scientific literature. And while the health manifestations of stress can be difficult to quantify, they are very real and highly significant.

Give Yourself a RAISE clearly lays out a money management system and provides a financial plan with the admirable goal of reducing your financial stress. In these difficult economic times, financial stress will undoubtedly play an even greater role in all of our lives. I applaud Mr. Bennett's efforts in helping readers regain control of their financial lives. This may be the best prescription for a healthy and happy future.

CHAPTER TWO

Objectives, Plans, Goals, and Budgets

Managing your financial life is much like planning a vacation. The first step is to set a specific destination or objective. For a vacation, your objective may be a place. It is clear when you get there that you have arrived at the place you intended to be. Your financial "destination" is not likely to be as clear and unambiguous as a geographic place, so you have to go to some lengths to define where you intend to be financially so you will know when you have arrived. Financial freedom is a great objective. Now you need to define success.

Once you have an objective, you need a plan. If your vacation is Disney World, you have choices on how to get there. Do you want to fly, drive, or take the train? A plan focuses on the "how-to-do-it." Assume you are a two-income family. Your plan may be to live on a single income and use the other income to pay off debt or invest for the future.

Goals are part of the plan, and we will spend time setting goals in Chapter 4.

Lastly, budgets are the final small steps for implementing the plans.

You do not need to program every penny of every dollar to achieve financial freedom any more than you need to have a plan for every minute of every day of your vacation trip. Within broad plans you can adapt as you go. But anything left to chance alone has a much lower probability of being successful.

On some occasions, it may be okay to hop in the car, head off in any direction, and hope that you will find a room at the end of the day and in the process have some fun. Most of us need more structure than that. Likewise with your money, a deliberate process will lead you more assuredly to financial freedom than just spending randomly.

In Chapter 1, you assessed your current financial freedom risk by taking a short quiz. How do you want your risk to be different in the future?

Financial Freedom

Financial freedom is when you have complete control over your money in both the short term and the long term. That is, cash in your pocket is completely within your control. You are free to keep it or spend it on anything that pleases you. But once you have spent it, you have exercised your choice forever. Financial freedom is also lost when you promise future money to someone else by borrowing and going into debt. So the key question you must answer for yourself is "How much financial freedom do I want to give up?"

Objectives

Because you are reading this book, I assume that your objectives are to achieve what the title promises: You want to "give yourself a raise, have more money, less stress, and financial freedom."

Why Do You Really Want or Need a Raise?

The most common answer to "Why do you want a raise?" is "I want (or need) more cash." That seems simple enough. But what you will do with more cash? The basic choices are to:

1. **Change your life style.** You want to buy more stuff or do more than you can do now with the amount of cash coming in.

2. **Get out of debt.** You want to pay off charges for past stuff or activities that you charged on credit instead of paying cash at the time of purchase.

3. **Save and invest.** You want to set aside more for the future so you can retire comfortably.

You may want to do all three of the preceding, but the list pretty much summarizes the choices.

The objectives I advocate for maximum financial freedom are to (1) maintain control of your finances, (2) live within your means (which means free of debt), and (3) set aside money to prepare for the future.

The underlying idea in *Give Yourself a RAISE* is that money you are now wasting can be rescued and is "found" money. In effect, stopping waste gives you a raise, and you can best accomplish this by having a financial plan.

Plans

Successful money management requires a plan. Without a plan, money flows in and money flows out and when the month or year is over you are left wondering, "Where did all that money go?" Plans route your money to predetermined uses. Plans are the big-picture strategy.

Before I discuss a system for managing money day to day (Chapter 6), let's examine a really simple general plan. Once you have a plan, then you can plug in the numbers to carry it out.

The "60 Percent Solution"

Richard Jenkins, editor-in-chief of *MSN Money*, created the widely publicized "60 percent solution," which is an excellent way to get started. His plan calls for you to divide your income into five categories and then stick with the program.

- 10 percent investment/retirement—really long term.

- 10 percent long-term savings—money needed in 5-plus years (e.g., college fund).

- 10 percent short-term savings—irregular and emergency expenses (escrow expenses).

- 10 percent fun—dining out, movies, toys, vacations, and sanity essentials.

- 60 percent—everything else, including taxes.

You can access his plan and other useful information at http://money central.msn.com.

Some church-based budget programs are similar to the Jenkins plan but even simpler. Pay God first (tithing: 10 percent), pay yourself next (retirement set-aside: 10 percent), and live on the rest (80 percent). I know many people who follow this model, and none of them are financially stressed or living beyond their means. They are very happy and content.

Again, both of the preceding systems are mere guidelines for allocation of the total income stream. But whatever you decide about your money, the system you use to allocate the money needs to be simple in order for it to work reliably for you. A simple and virtually foolproof bank-account-based system is the subject of Chapter 6.

Right now perhaps you cannot live on the 60 percent in the Jenkins plan. You may need more than the 60 percent, and therefore something in one of Jenkins' other categories will have to change to a lower percentage. But over the long haul, you may want to strive to reach the 60 percent goal. You now have a target toward which to work.

As an example, refer to Illustration 2.1 to see how the 60 percent model would look for a person with an annual total income of $60,000, or $5,000 a month.

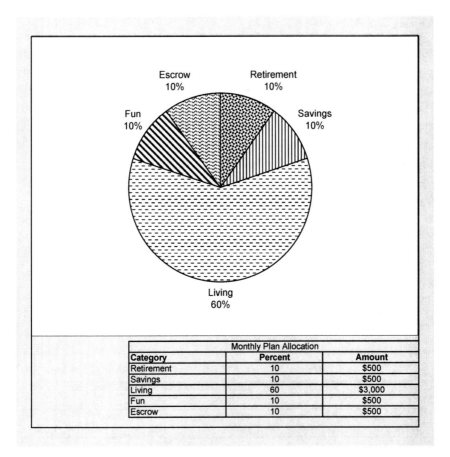

Monthly Plan Allocation		
Category	**Percent**	**Amount**
Retirement	10	$500
Savings	10	$500
Living	60	$3,000
Fun	10	$500
Escrow	10	$500

Illustration 2.1   The Jenkins Plan, $5,000 Gross Income per Month

Make Your Own Plan

Now, try this exercise for yourself. First, fill in your gross monthly income on the line below. Then, list the uses to which you would *like* to allocate your income—broken into *10 percent* increments. I've chosen 10 percent because this approach allows you to break down Jenkins' 60 percent segment into smaller chunks, some of which may certainly vary over time. Of course, it is fine to use more than one 10 percent increment for the same category if that fits your situation. Remember when filling out the following form that these figures represent your desired plan for future spending, not necessarily your present spending.

Monthly gross income estimate: $ _____

Percent	Use of Income by Category	Target Amount
10		
10		
10		
10		
10		
10		
10		
10		
10		
10		

Finally, write in your categories on the blank pie chart (Illustration 2.2) and label the segments with the percentage and your estimated monthly dollar allocation to that category. (Blank pie charts also appear on my Web site, www.ptff.net. Download the Excel file, enter your numbers into it, and try several variations.). When you've filled in this pie chart, you have a picture of what your financial target looks like.

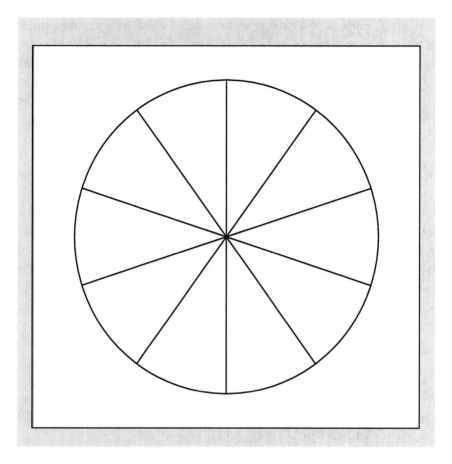

Illustration 2.2   Blank Chart with 10 Percent Segments

Later, in Chapter 3, when you are gathering data on your recent financial history, you can refine these target numbers. You will be able to compare what the actual numbers are (from your own real data) to what you want the targets to be.

This exercise forces you to face reality. If you cannot live within the income-use categories you define, something will have to change.

This is a very quick and very simple plan that may work for you.

Goals

Goals are specific. Chapter 4 is all about goals. Objectives and plans are the big-picture overview of your intended financial life, but goals detail exactly what you want to achieve within that framework. Goals are the details of where the allocations of chunks of money get spent in the short term and in the long term.

Goals really help control impulse spending because they focus your activity on predetermined priorities.

Budgets (or Spending Plans)

The mere mention of the word *budget* evokes a range of responses from terror to indifference. As with dieting, everybody has an experience—usually bad—with the failure of this or that budget program.

Two schools of thought dominate the budget discussion. Traditionalists insist on penny-by-penny allocation for anything and everything. Experience suggests that this approach is short lived. Like the diet that has a person weighing each half ounce of every portion, the effort of allocating every penny seems misplaced and discouraging. Most people who try traditional budgets quit after a very short time.

The alternative budget approach is to "chunk" money into categories and then allow the spender discretion to mete out the funds over a given time period. Take a weekly allowance as an example. Suppose Mary gets $100 for the week to cover her lunches, dry cleaning, personal items, and incidental expenses. What need is there to plot out a day-by-day plan down to the magazine, cup of coffee, and pack of chewing gum? Mary will instinctively hoard enough money early in the week to make it through until Friday without the necessity of a written plan. She may even carry forward some extra so she can splurge next week. She will know when she is out of money, provided there is no ATM or credit card option as a bailout.

In the chunk budget method, money may also be budgeted for specific uses (including such things as goals and getting out of debt).

As you progress through this book, you can make your budget as chunky or detailed as fits your own needs. There is no right way, only a way that works for you.

How Detailed Does a Budget Need to Be?

Most paper-trail budgets bog down in very small details and involve too much record keeping. Since this is the case, you need to minimize the detail but do so to an extent consistent with keeping enough control to know that you are on track.

The amount of detail required in a plan is directly related to (1) how many people are involved in the plan and (2) how complicated their lives are—that is, how many bills are there to be paid?

For a solo individual, it is possible to live without even having a bank account. Get paid, pay cash for everything, spend until the money is gone, and survive to the next payday. Millions of people live that way.

When life becomes more complicated and there are bills to be paid that are not practical to pay in cash (like the rent and utilities), the plan needs to accommodate these regular items. When more than one person is involved, the spending plan needs to change to meet the different needs. As you will see, the system I outline never gets outdated or obsolete. Additional pieces are simply added as complexity increases.

History and Forecasting

In all likelihood, you have only a vague notion of where your money goes by category. We have lived in prosperous times that have created the impression that we need not be careful with our money. "Easy come, easy go" was something I remember my grandmother saying. Right now more and more people are seeing the "easy come" part changing, and therefore need a very accurate sense of just how the money is being spent.

Chapter 3 is devoted to showing you how to gather historical data so you will know where you have been spending your money and can then make necessary changes to carry out your spending plan. As you'll see from the guidelines in Chapter 3, when you gather this historical data, you will want as much detail as possible.

Forecasting is *guessing* (sorry, but even for the experts that is what forecasting really is) about the future and *planning* to do things differently, again to match your actions to your plan. If, for example, you agree with Jenkins that 10 percent is a good allocation for "fun" and your analysis shows you actually spent 16 percent for fun last year, you can plan to change next year. You might "forecast" 12 percent instead.

With a plan in place, forecasting is simply anticipating the future and matching your spending to your intent.

Some Accounting Basics

In discussing money, inevitably accounting jargon will creep in, and it is important to understand a few basic terms.

The terms *money* and *cash* are too narrow for the purposes of this book. To avoid confusion, in this book the term *funds* will be used to mean "all resources that are used in purchasing transactions."

The term **source** *of funds* is usually thought of as *income*, and source of funds refers to everything that can be used to pay for something. It includes wages, investment income, savings, sale of assets, gifts, and loans (credit cards, auto loans, mortgages, etc.).

The term **use** *of funds* refers to what was acquired (or repaid) with the source of funds (income).

The source of funds must always equal the use of funds. In other words, everything is paid for in some way.

If you are using more funds than you are currently earning from working wages or investments, either you are selling off assets (like cashing in a certificate of deposit (CD), selling a car, or taking cash out of savings) or you are borrowing and going deeper into debt. In any case, the source of funds (wages and money generated from selling off assets or new borrowing) over any period of time will always exactly equal the use of funds (money spent for things or debt reduction and savings/investments).

Funds coming in can be used to pay for current purchases, pay off previous debts, or increase your assets (more savings, for example.)

Net worth is another piece of accounting jargon that you will encounter any time you start looking at your financial picture.

So far we have been discussing a "flow" of funds, sources of funds, and uses of funds over a period of time—usually one month or one year. Net worth (NW) is a snapshot of a single point of time. It simply is the difference, expressed in dollars, between what you own and what you owe at that instant.

For example, if you have a home worth $200,000, a car worth $15,000, and $35,000 in savings, you have assets (what you own) totaling $250,000. But you still owe $165,000 on your home mortgage and $10,000 on your car, for total liabilities (what you owe) of $175,000. Your net worth is your assets ($250,000) minus your liabilities ($175,000), or NW = $75,000.

As you can see, any activity with your funds changes your net worth.

For more understanding of personal financial net worth, you are encouraged to read one of the many fundamentals books available or do a Google search for "personal net worth."

Summary

Before moving on, quickly review where you are and where you are headed and assume that you intend something along the following lines:

- My *objective* is to maximize my financial freedom by living within my means, staying out of debt, and setting aside funds for the future.

- My *plan* for reaching my objectives is to limit my day-to-day expenses to 60 percent of my gross income.

- My *specific goals* will be written out (Chapter 4).

- I will create a *more detailed plan (or budget)* to manage my day-to-day financial activities, monitor my success, and keep me in control (Chapter 5).

With the fundamentals clearly in mind, you are now ready to proceed with collecting a history of your sources of funds and uses of funds.

Fast-Track Option

Look back at your financial freedom Final Risk Score from Chapter 1. If you scored well (a high number of risk points), you may wish to skip the next chapters on gathering financial history, setting goals, and forecasting. You can go directly to Chapter 6, which describes how to use the Freedom Money Management System™ of electronic banking and multiple bank accounts.

However, I strongly recommend the activities in Chapters 3, 4, and 5. Gathering a detailed history of your past habits, setting goals, and forecasting future spending patterns are excellent discipline, even if you are not financially stressed. These exercises are an opportunity for a very good review of your finances and will force you to think about your personal priorities.

Myth   Budgeting doesn't work. I have tried it and in a month or two I am right back to my old habits and am out of control.

Fact   Budgets rarely work; a basic spending plan can. Most people abandon a highly detailed budget within a very short period. The problem is simply that you cannot predict with any degree of consistent accuracy what your spending needs (or whims) will be. You can make gross assumptions and then control your spending from period to period.

Solution   Allocate chunks of money rather than tiny little amounts. Start using cash instead of plastic. If you have only $50 in your pocket to last until the end of the month, you are perfectly capable on a day-to-day basis of deciding whether or not to indulge in a $4.95 cup of coffee. Some days you will and some days you won't, as your urges vary.

Myth   I can get someone to do a plan for me.

Fact   Nobody cares more about you than you care about yourself. You have to do your own planning. It is an excellent idea to get all of the help and guidance you can, but it has to be your values and your plan or it will never work for you.

Solution   Start right now. Using your goals, promise yourself that you will complete a plan by a certain date—a date close enough to create some urgency but far enough out to be realistic.

CHAPTER THREE

History and Forecasting

Why You Need to Look Back Before You Plan Ahead

If your Final Risk Score from the Financial Freedom Risk Assessment quiz in Chapter 1 is lower than you want it to be—if your financial risk is greater than you are comfortable with—it is time to make changes in how you manage your money.

The first truth is that you cannot continue managing your money the same way you have been and expect different results. An increasing financial risk will not correct itself, and if simply ignored the risk will probably worsen.

Before you can change and improve your habits, you must do some basic research to get an accurate picture of exactly where your money has been going. After completing this "money homework," you may be able to improve your financial situation by modifying only a few things, particularly if you have a good income, are living within your means, and have a high Financial Freedom Risk profile. Or, if you are facing the results of years of out-of-control spending, borrowing, and living large, more dramatic measures may be required over a relatively long period to get back in control of your money life.

Two separate components make up your money life: (1) Money coming in (income, or "sources of funds") and (2) money going out (expenses, or "uses of funds"). If more money is coming in than going out, you probably feel pretty good. If more money is going out than coming in, you are going into debt.

Money problems (or dissatisfactions) can be solved only by bringing more money into your life or by reducing the amount going out—or a combination of the two. No other choices exist! The purpose of this book is to teach you how to do both.

An accurate picture of the past will help you craft a sensible program for the future. This chapter is a guide to help you gather that history and organize it into useful modules. The intent is to identify opportunities for changing your spending habits to eliminate waste. Unnecessary spending that is eliminated becomes money over which you have discretion, and you will thereby give yourself a raise.

When you finish the activities in this chapter, you will have gathered, analyzed, and recorded data on your income history (Form 3.1) and expense history (Forms 3.2–3.6) and compared income/expense data to identify your spending patterns (Form 3.7). (Forms with sample data appear throughout this chapter, and blank forms appear at the end of the chapter and can be found on my Web site, www.ptff.net.) In Chapter 5, you will use this data to formulate a personal spending plan.

Building a Financial History Database

Building a history database and planning the future is a five-step process:

1. Gather last year's data

2. Organize the data into categories

3. Analyze your spending

4. Identify areas for change

5. Plan the future

Why Bother?

Looking at "money in" and "money out" may seem a tedious and time-consuming process, but the benefits are enormous. I promise, you will be surprised at how many little things add up over a year's time. I was at a workshop where one woman tallied the cost of buying diet cola at the vending machines where she worked and was startled to discover that in one year she was spending over $1,700. And another woman confided that she and her husband spent $9.83 every day on cigarettes. That is an annual habit of nearly $3,600. A friend was surprised that she spent over $300 a month on lattes.

The purpose of the process of looking at spending patterns is not to make moral judgments. It is your money. Spend it freely (and, one hopes, wisely). But with accurate figures, you can decide whether the pleasure is worth the cost. Remember, you are looking for the leaks in your money bucket.

Gathering Historical Income and Spending Data

Gathering data can be a very simple task if you have mountains of well-organized, detailed records and receipts. If, however, your record keeping is like that of many people, gathering data may be a real challenge. You can expect to spend considerable time doing it, but the understanding of your habits will be worthwhile.

Start by assembling all of your financial records from last year. These records should include your income records, checking account statements, mortgage statements, credit card and other charge account statements, miscellaneous receipts, and anything else that gives you a detailed record of where your money came from and where it was spent. Include a copy of last year's income tax filing.

After you have gathered every available document that can help you construct a historical record of "where did all that money go," organize it into useful categories.

Chances are that you will not have a paper trail for everything you spent. There will be a huge gap between the total amount of money you brought in and what you can account for as having been spent. Filling in this information gap is part of the challenge and is what makes this part of the process time-consuming.

It is in the area of "I have no idea where that money went!" that the potential for identifying waste is highest. After all, if you do not know what you spent the money for, how important can it be? Try guessing. Or just have a category labeled as "I don't know." It's not worth your time looking for every penny spent in the past. It is worthwhile to have a sound plan for the future—so find as much detail as necessary to help you do that.

Even if your records are thin, you can still gain an idea of your actual spending by doing the one-month detailed analysis described at the end of this chapter and then estimating overall spending from that.

Recommendation: Start with the easy things and focus on the big picture. Try not to get bogged down in details until you have decided you really need to go to a more detailed level. If you first try to sort things down to the smallest items, you may get discouraged and be tempted to give up. But abandoning the data-gathering process is not a good idea.

Organizing Your Data into Categories

One big pile of receipts and records is not very useful. The next step is to sort the information you have into logical categories that work for you.

First separate your data into an income pile and an expense pile. Your personal life circumstances will decide how much detail (how much further sorting) each pile requires.

Income Sort

If you work for one employer who pays you a regular paycheck and you have no other income, your income pile is pretty small. If you are a freelance contract worker, are self-employed, have worked for several people, or have a wide variety of income sources, your income pile is a bit larger.

A factor that complicates income tabulation is that employment records include not only income but also items withheld from your paycheck, which in reality are expense items or investments such as 401(k) contributions (all of which must be included in your analysis of spending). In the following pages, I'll describe the "ins" and "outs" of capturing income data accurately.

Suggested Expense Categories

Spend some time just thinking about categories into which your expenses logically fall before you start writing anything down. To help you decide on the categories that best fit your situation, I find five major categories useful for planning, and they appear in the sample forms in this chapter.

1. Regular monthly fixed expenses (Form 3.2)

2. Regular monthly variable expenses (Form 3.3)

3. Discretionary expenses (Form 3.4)

4. Irregular/predictable expenses (Form 3.5)

5. Interest and fees paid (Form 3.6)

I offer the preceding five broad categories of expense as a starting point, but you should feel free to tailor expense categories to fit your own circumstances. The main point is to analyze your spending and sort it into meaningful modules (later in the chapter forms will be provided to facilitate the sort). Once you break down your spending, you have a readymade tool for identifying leaks in your spending bucket. Plug the leaks and you'll give yourself a raise!

1. Expenses: Regular Monthly Fixed Amounts

Regular monthly *fixed* expenses are those that are paid every month in the same amount *without the option of skipping the payment.* Three examples are items deducted from your paycheck, your rent or mortgage payment, and your automobile loan.

2. Expenses: Regular Monthly Variable Amounts

Regular monthly *variable* expenses are those that you have to pay every month but *the amount may vary each month.* These are expenses that you must pay but are never quite sure what the amounts will be. Groceries, fuel, and utility bills are typical monthly variable expenses.

For most people, credit card statements will be a prime source of information about monthly variable expenses. But you must further break down a credit card bill into categories of purchases to understand where the money is going. Each credit card statement likely has items in various categories such as groceries, recreation, car repairs, or home maintenance. Also, if you don't pay off your entire balance each month, a credit card statement probably includes interest charges and fees, which are an expense category.

3. Expenses: Discretionary

Discretionary expenses are those that can be put off from month to month. They may be mandatory, but they provide you with the options of when and how much will be paid or spent. Routine dental care, car maintenance, entertainment, and gifts are examples. Again, breaking down credit card statements will be a gold mine of detailed information about your discretionary spending, but you'll have to take the time to analyze the items on the bill.

It's worth taking a hard look at discretionary expenses because spending "leaks" and opportunities to revise your spending habits are often found within this category. It is also the area where you are least likely to be able to analyze where the money went.

Three subcategories may help with the process.

1. **Joint or family items:** These are items that the whole family shares— such as eating out, gifts, donations, and other services rendered to the whole family (like house cleaning or yard maintenance). Savings and investments (other than those being deducted automatically from your paycheck) are in this category.

2. **Personal items for each member of the family (think allowances):** These can be identified with one spender and may include commuting expenses, personal grooming, lunches, clothing, lessons, sports participation, and so on.

3. **Recreation and leisure:** This category is separate for a reason. It is essential for a healthy and happy existence to program in some fun. A reasonable amount to spend in this category is 10 percent of gross income. Some spend far more than this and others are far too frugal. By sorting out this expense, you can assess your own habits.

Make your own subcategories to fit your life style and preferences.

4. Expenses: Irregular/Predictable (To Be Escrowed)

An escrow is an amount set aside for an upcoming event. For example, if you have a home mortgage, the lender may include a sum (an escrow) in your monthly payment that will accumulate enough extra money to pay insurance and property taxes when they are due.

Irregular expenses are those that occur other than monthly and are often large amounts not easily paid from regular monthly income. Property taxes, additional income taxes, insurance premiums (car insurance, home insurance, and so on), school tuition, car repairs, and emergencies fit this category.

You are probably well aware of your own irregular expenses from previous experience because they become budget busters and require some money juggling.

5. Interest and Fees Paid

Interest is a charge paid for the use of money. For example, when you buy something with a credit card and do not pay the total amount of the credit card bill each month, the card company charges you interest on the balance of the bill. Similarly, when you take out a loan to buy something like a home or car, the lender loans you the money to pay for the whole item and then charges you interest to pay off that loan month by month. Interest increases the ultimate cost of anything you buy on credit.

When analyzing your finances on the forms in this chapter, record interest twice: The primary entry for interest is with the bill itself (on one of the expense forms); the secondary entry for interest is on the "Summary of Interest and Fees Paid" form. I suggest using this separate "Interest and Fees" form because it is important to know how much money you are paying someone else that simply increases the cost of everything for you. When you get out of debt, eliminating interest payments is a real raise for you. (Note that car payment statements often fail to break out interest separately, so don't worry if you can't track down that interest figure.)

Where Do I Put . . . ?

By now you have discovered that some expenses can go in two or more different places. There are no hard and fast rules. Do what makes sense for your situation, but be consistent. The forms in this chapter contain possible categories for some common items. Use them as a starting point but feel free to add and amend categories to meet your own needs. Once you have decided on your own category organization, write down the details for future reference and planning and be consistent.

You may at this point find it useful to review the sample blank forms (blanks of Forms 3.1 through 3.7 appear at the end of this chapter) before you start recording your own. Also, three cautions relevant to filling out forms are in order before you dig into the process of sorting and categorizing your data.

Cautions About Filling out Forms in This Chapter

Caution 1: About Credit Cards

A credit card is both (1) a tool for borrowing (that is, it is a source of "funds") and (2) a method of paying for stuff (that is, through it you pay for "expenses"). These two facets of credit cards make organizing your data a bit more complex, but it is vital to correctly understand the functions of credit cards to see how they affect your financial life.

Credit Cards as a "Source of Funds"

When you use a credit card, the card allows you to buy more now than you can afford to pay for now by borrowing from the credit card company. That is, the credit card has become another source of funds, just like any other loan but at a usually exorbitant interest rate.

When you gather your income data, you will see that Form 3.1, "Source of Funds," has a line for "Credit card, increased balance." *Increased credit card balance* is defined as the difference between your outstanding balance at the beginning of any period and the outstanding balance at the end of the same period.

For example, if on January 1 your credit card had a balance owing of $4,500 and on December 31 the balance owing was $9,000, the credit card increase of $4,500 is a *source of funds*. The $4,500 is the amount you have borrowed in that year.

Credit Cards as a Method of Payment

In and of themselves, credit cards are not a single "category" of expense; fundamentally, a credit card is one *method of paying* for goods or services and getting cash; that is, do not record a total credit card payment as just one bill. You'll need to look over your credit card statements and categorize the line items on the statement. Here's how a credit card statement breaks down:

1. On any one monthly credit card statement you may have a utility bill, groceries, doctor bills, dining out, dry cleaning, gasoline, car repairs, department store charges, and so on, which fall into a variety

of expense categories. These items need to be sorted into categories of expense (which you will record on Forms 3.2–3.5 as appropriate).

2. Also, if you do not pay your entire balance each month, you have finance (or interest) charges and perhaps even late fees or penalties. These charges are expenses and should be recorded primarily on the "Discretionary Expenses" form (Form 3.5).

3. Finally, you may, unfortunately (the cost is high), obtain an outright loan from your credit card as a cash advance, or you may use one of those tempting blank checks the credit card companies send out to get you deeper in debt. By offering these features, the credit card companies are definitely not looking out for you! Cash obtained from a credit card is simply another source of funds. It is not an expense.

Caution 2: Avoid Double Counting

As you analyze your documents, you may have a record of the same transaction in more than one place, so be careful that you do not count the same item twice. For example, you may have a physical receipt from Texaco for gasoline and a charge on your credit card statement from Texaco for the same purchase. Count that Texaco purchase only once.

Interest charges are the only exception to this. When you pay interest on something (a house loan, credit card), you should record that interest in its appropriate expense category (Forms 3.2–3.5) and also record it on a separate form devoted only to interest (Form 3.6). The only function of this "Summary of Interest and Fees Paid" form is to tally interest and make you focus on just how big a raise you could give yourself if you eliminated some or all interest payments from your life.

Some interest is easy to isolate. A monthly home mortgage statement usually has an allocation to principal and interest. Credit card interest or finance charges are always stated separately. However, the interest on a car loan is embedded in the monthly payment and cannot easily be separated out. Disclosure documents at the time of the loan will show the total amount of interest that you will pay over the life of the car loan. For the purposes of gathering history, it is not worth the effort to track down the interest on your car loan.

For planning and forecasting, you may want to consider the entire amount of your monthly car payments as an opportunity to save money in the future by paying off the loan on your car and paying cash for the next car.

Caution 3: Some Receipts Have Items in Several Categories

As you proceed with your data collection and categorization, some receipts (like ones from department stores) may have items that fall into a variety of categories. To really find out where your money is going, you'll need to sort out items into their various categories. For example, you may have a receipt from a store like Target with quite a few items, which fall into a variety of categories (some groceries, some personal, some entertainment, etc.). Later in the chapter, I've included a couple of annotated store receipts as samples to give you an idea how to treat such receipts (Illustrations 3.8 and 3.9).

Recording Historical Data

Now make a set of forms on which you can record income sources (Form 3.1), various kinds of expenses (Forms 3.2–3.6), and a summary form tallying the two (Form 3.7). This chapter contains samples of such forms, but you should amend the samples to reflect your own circumstances. Blanks of forms shown in this chapter appear at the end of the chapter, or you can download full-size blank forms from our Web site:

www.ptff.net

The seven sample forms included are:

- Form 3.1: Source of Funds

- Form 3.2: Expenses: Regular Monthly Fixed Amounts

- Form 3.3: Expenses: Regular Monthly Variable Amounts

- Form 3.4: Expenses: Discretionary

- Form 3.5: Expenses: Irregular/Predictable (To Be Escrowed)

- Form 3.6: Summary of Interest and Fees Paid

- Form 3.7: Source and Use of Funds Summary

I recommend that each of your forms have two sections: "History" (a record of the past data) and "Forecast" (what you expect to happen in the future). By collecting past data and simultaneously looking ahead, you can begin to see very quickly where there are opportunities (or needs) for change.

The process of gathering your historical spending record, setting future goals (which is covered in detail in Chapter 4), and forecasting individual spending categories (Chapter 5) is very much trial-and-error, particularly if your past history has been loose and unfocused. It may take a while for you to get used to becoming more specific with your money. With a big-picture plan, adding here and taking away there is a balancing act, but constant revising is inevitable and healthy.

About the Filled-in Examples of Forms (Illustrations)

The forms provided in this book are simple and self-explanatory, but because some readers will find examples of filled-in forms helpful, in some cases I have provided filled-in sample forms (hereafter called *illustrations*).

A Few Important Points

- The sample forms are not what is important. You can easily create your own forms to fit your preferences. What is important is that you have some type of a system to plan and keep track of your financial activities.

- The samples are not integrated. That is, there is no absolute link between chapters and the examples used. Do not waste your time trying to reconcile the examples. Just grasp the concepts and apply them to your own circumstances. These are not recommended guidelines, just examples.

- There are only two rules: (1) Pay yourself first and (2) stay out of debt. How you divide up the money coming in and how you account for it is simply technique. Do what works for you and do something that is comfortable and practical for you.

The Fictitious Johnson Family

This chapter uses fictitious data about the Johnson family of four—father, Joe; mother, Sue; and children John (13) and Shelley (10)—in some of the illustrations.

Joe—accountant, yearly gross salary	$54,000
Sue—part-time medical office receptionist	$18,000
Combined income	$72,000

Joe currently has only contributed 2 percent of his gross salary to his 401(k). The company will match his contribution 50 percent up to 6 percent of his salary. He wants to raise his contribution, but the Johnsons are currently spending everything they make.

They own a home with a monthly mortgage payment of $880, and they have a five-year car loan of $250 per month. Sue drives an older car, which is paid for.

The family takes a one-week yearly vacation. With transportation, food, and entertainment, they typically spend $4,500. Joe also enjoys baseball and purchases tickets for the family for five games every year. Including food, this costs $1,250. Sue enjoys going to movies and so they go out once a month. Tickets, popcorn, drinks, and candy average $60, for a yearly total cost of $720.

With two children, they have a busy life, and often it is difficult to cook and get the family to sit down for dinner. So it is not surprising that they frequently eat takeout pizza, Chinese, or burgers, for which they spend about $500 a month.

The children both get allowances to use as they like. Joe goes out to lunch each day at work and often stops at the deli in his office building for coffee and bagels in the morning. He spends $400 a month.

Sue loves to shop, particularly for gifts for other people in her family. She buys the children new clothes for school each year and also enjoys buying presents for birthdays and Christmas, not only for the four of them but for the extended family of sisters, brothers, nieces, and nephews.

They know they should be saving more, particularly for college for the kids, but it seems so hard to make it with what they have. Much to their dismay, the balance on their credit cards increased by $3,000 last year, mostly due to the ball games, and Sue has started using the credit card to pay for groceries and other things since she is often out of money.

Studying the sample forms and reflecting on the challenges of the Johnson family may give you some ideas about how you can restructure your own financial life.

Guidelines for Completing the Chapter 3 Forms

Sources of Funds (Form 3.1)

The beginning point in any money planning process is to identify every source of money available or expected to become available. On Form 3.1, "Sources of Funds," record *all* sources of funds received in the past year. Identify when or how often each was received and whether you expect to receive it this year.

Monthly or Annual Income? One or More Earners?

Not every form of income is a regular monthly amount. For monthly items, multiply by 12 to get the annual figure. For irregular income, just enter the total annual amount.

If your household has more than one wage earner, each person's income should be recorded separately. Make a separate Form 3.1 for each wage earner, fill out the forms, and then add the figures together from the separate forms and record on a summary Form 3.1.

Income Categories

The following is a brief description of typical income categories to use in documenting your sources of income on Form 3.1.

Current income: The gross (or total) amounts of wages or salary, commissions, overtime, bonuses, part-time work, or freelance/contract income are in this category.

Investments: Interest received from savings or bonds, dividends, annuities, pensions, retirement payments, Social Security payments are in this category.

Asset sale/redemption: Selling your house, car, or investments; cashing in maturing certificates of deposit (CDs) or closing out a savings account; and holding a garage sale or eBay auction of unused stuff are sources of cash.

Windfalls: Tax refunds, inheritances, gifts, lottery or gambling winnings, insurance settlements, and the like are in this category.

Increased debt: When all of the above sources of income are inadequate, what remains is borrowing. Loans, increased credit card balances, home equity lines of credit, payday loans, buying something with "no money

Form 3.1   Sources of Funds

Item	History			Forecast		
	When received	Amount		When received	Amount	
CURRENT INCOME		Monthly	Annual		Monthly	Annual
Wages/Salary: Gross pay [Joe]		4500	54000			
Payroll deductions are listed on Form 3-2 as regular monthly fixed expenses.						
Commissions						
Overtime						
Bonuses						
Part-time income [Sue]		1500	18000			
Other:						
Total Current Income		6000	72000			
INVESTMENTS						
Interest Received						
Dividends						
Annuities						
Pension or retirement payout						
Social Security						
Other:						
Total Investment Income			0			
ASSET SALE/Redemption						
Stock/bond sale proceeds						
Savings Withdrawal						
CDs maturing						
Sale of other assets						
Total Asset Proceeds			0			
WINDFALLS						
Tax refund						
Gifts/Inheritances						
Other (specify)						
Total Windfall			0			
DEBT INCREASE						
Credit card, increased balance			3000			
Home equity loan or credit line						
Refinance home						
Personal loans						
Installment purchases						
Borrowing from retirement funds						
Other						
Total Debt Increase			3000			
Total Source of Funds			75000			

Illustration 3.1   Form 3.1 with Sample Data

down," borrowing from your retirement funds, and loans from family are all examples of increased debt as a source of funds.

Identifying increased debt amounts is fairly simple. For example, say you had a balance brought forward on a credit card of $6,000 on January 1, and on December 31 you have an ending balance of $10,000; you would have $4,000 in increased credit card debt for the year.

Illustration 3.1 shows Form 3.1 with some sample data. A blank of Form 3.1 appears at the end of the chapter.

Expenses: Regular Monthly Fixed Amounts (Form 3.2)

Payroll Deductions

If you receive a regular paycheck, your employer probably makes deductions from your paycheck. These deductions should be listed as expenses on Form 3.2. Paycheck deductions fall into several categories: taxes, personal expenses, investments/savings, and loans.

1. **Taxes (federal, state, local, Social Security)** withheld from your paycheck reduce your pay. The money is credited against your ultimate tax liability. Some people think it is a good idea to withhold more taxes than you will ultimately owe so you will get a nice refund check at tax time. They see this as a sort of forced savings plan or vacation account. Excess withholding is not a good idea for a couple of reasons. Excess tax withheld from your paycheck earns no interest. Why "lend" the government your money interest free? If you are having trouble making ends meet, excess withholding may deprive you of a source of cash that can keep you from going into debt. If you want to force yourself to save, have your payroll department put money into an interest-bearing savings account automatically instead of giving it to the government as withheld taxes.

   Remember, enter the amounts of taxes withheld on Form 3.2 as fixed expenses. They are fixed expenses because you do not have any choice about having them deducted monthly (except that you do have some discretion over the amount you elect to have withheld).

2. **Investments** deducted from your paycheck, such as 401(k) contributions, should also be entered on Form 3.2 as a fixed expense. Of course, you can decide to stop an investment deduction, but for as long as an investment is automatically being withheld, treat it as a fixed expense. Later, when you formulate a spending plan with a savings goal, show the method of paying such an investment as a payroll deduction.

3. **Personal expenses** that are withheld should also be entered on Form 3.2. Your group insurance contribution is such an expense. When you are drawing up a spending plan, you will show that it is paid by a deduction from your paycheck, not from your net pay.

4. **Loan payments** are another typical deduction. For example, you may finance your car through the company credit union, and the payments are automatically deducted from your pay. Or you may have borrowed from your 401(k), and those loan payments are deducted from your pay. Enter the amounts on Form 3.2.

Other Regular Fixed Amounts

Anything that must be paid every month in the same amount without the option of skipping the payment is in this category. Regular monthly fixed expenses include, in addition to payroll deductions, such things as mortgage or rent payments and automobile loans. (Remember to include a loan's total payment on Form 3.2, but also record a loan's interest on Form 3.6.) Utility bills vary month to month, but if your electric company or fuel oil company offers a 12-month plan to spread payments evenly over the year, those bills would go on Form 3.2. Insurance companies may have a similar plan.

Illustration 3.2 shows Form 3.2 with some sample data. A blank of Form 3.2 appears at the end of the chapter.

Form 3.2   Expenses: Regular Monthly Fixed Amounts

Item	When Paid	History Monthly	History Annually	Forecast Monthly	Forecast Annually
Payroll Deductions					
Federal income tax		600	7200		
State income tax					
Local income tax					
Social Security		330	3960		
Retirement contribution (401k)		90	1080		
Insurance		250	3000		
Loan payments					
Other					
Mortgage/Rent		880	10560		
Automobile Loan(s)		250	3000		
Other Loans					
Other					
Total Current Regular Fixed Expenses		2400	28800		

Note: The full payments for loans should be entered on this form. Wherever possible to identify the interest amount enter that on form 3.6 as well.

Illustration 3.2   Form 3.2 with Some Sample Data

Expenses: Regular Monthly Variable Amounts (Form 3.3)

Typical expenses in the monthly variable category include utility bills (gas, electric, phone, cable, cell phone); bank interest, service charges, and fees; and anything else that is billed regularly where the amount changes from month to month. These are expenses that you must pay once monthly but can never be quite sure how much the amount will be.

Credit Cards, a Special Case

As I noted earlier, credit card bills present a special case of variable monthly expense. A credit card is not an expense category, other than the fees and interest related to it. Credit cards are simply a way to pay for something. You must sort the items on each credit card statement into expense categories.

First, since credit card interest and fees are a variable monthly expense, record them on Form 3.3 and also record them on Form 3.6 (this form is designed to focus your attention on how much total interest you are paying).

Next, tackle categorizing the rest of the line items on the statement. A credit card statement may have items from many categories such as groceries, medical bills, clothing purchases, recreation, car repairs, or home maintenance. Most of these items will be either a monthly variable expense or a discretionary expense. You decide the category, but be consistent. Remember the guidelines—if a bill must be paid no matter what, but the amount varies, it is in the monthly variable category; if it can be postponed, it is a discretionary expense. Do not record the total credit card payment (the total credit card bill) itself as an expense; instead you are recording all the bill's component line items. If you record both the total credit card payment and all the line items, you will be double counting.

When you review your credit card statement, you will see line items that you cannot identify. Do not ignore these "what in the heck was this?" items. Total up such mysteries and enter them as "miscellaneous expenses" on the "Discretionary Expenses" form (Form 3.4). Mysteries are definitely a potential area for economizing!

Illustration 3.3 shows Form 3.3 ("Regular Monthly Variable Expenses") with some sample data. Blank Form 3.3 appears at the end of this chapter.

Form 3.3   Expenses: Regular Monthly Variable Amounts

Item	When paid	History Amount Monthly	Annually	Average/mo	Forecast Amount Monthly	Annually
Utilities						
Electrical		105	1260			
Gas/Oil		60	720			
Water		50	600			
Sewer			0			
Trash pick-up		20	240			
Cable		60	720			
Telephone (s)		45	540			
Cell phone		300	3600			
Food/Groceries		500	6000			
Transportation			0			
Automotive			0			
Fuel		170	2040			
Parking/tolls			0			
Insurance		200	2400			
Credit card interest *		70	840			
Bank charges			0			
Other			0			
Total Variable Monthly Expenses		1580	18960			

* Also enter the interest paid on form 3.6

Illustration 3.3   Form 3.3 with Sample Data

Expenses: Discretionary (Form 3.4)

Discretionary expenses are those that can be put off from month to month and the amounts of which may vary widely. Here is where serious analysis can really pay off. Spending "leaks" and opportunities to revise your spending habits are often found within this category. It is also the area where you are least likely to be able to analyze where the money went.

Personal items and allowances are clearly discretionary, as are most entertainment and recreation expenses. Savings and investments are discretionary, except for those you have set up to be automatic, such as a payroll deduction (which is a regular monthly fixed amount).

When analyzing your bank statements and check register and your credit card statements, remember that you will find items you are not sure how to categorize. Record those amounts as "miscellaneous," but do not forget them. They are a serious "leak" area.

Debt Reduction

The "Debt Reduction" line item or category on Form 3.4 is intended to identify and isolate reduction of debt that is not already accounted for elsewhere.

A home mortgage and an automobile loan payment both allocate a portion of the payment to the principal (which reduces the debt) and a portion to the interest. Since other line items (on Form 3.2) account for them as regular expenses, do not enter them here. The interest on the mortgage is easy to identify; the interest on an auto loan is not.

If, however, you choose to make an additional principal payment on any loan, this is where you record it. This line item is particularly useful when you are following the guidelines for getting out of debt in Chapter 7.

Debt reduction on credit cards is a little more complicated to record. If you have not made any new purchases on the credit card, the minimum payment covers the interest or finance charges and a small portion of the previous balance. If you make a substantial additional payment with the intent to get out of debt, that would be entered in this field.

If you have new purchases on a credit card, making a minimum payment will not likely reduce the previous balance, so simply distribute the charges to their appropriate category.

Remember, the purpose of all of these forms is not to build an elaborate and technically correct accounting document. They are meant to help you grasp the scope of your financial activities and manage them to meet your objectives.

Illustration 3.4 shows Form 3.4 with sample data. Blank Form 3.4 appears at the end of this chapter.

Form 3.4   Expenses: Discretionary

Item	Who pays	History Amount Monthly	History Amount Annual	Average/mo	Forecast Amount Monthly	Forecast Amount Annual
Personal Items						
Sue - Hair		30	360			
Sue - Clothes		65	780			
Kids - Clothes		85	1020			
Joe - Clothes		35	420			
Allowances			0			
John (13)		100	1200			
Shelley (10)		50	600			
Joe - lunch and coffee		400	4800			
			0			
Medical/Dental			0			
Medical		20	240			
			0			
Recreation/Entertainment			0			
Movies		60	720			
Eat out/Take out		500	6000			
			0			
Debt reduction *			0			
			0			
			0			
			0			
Other			0			
Gifts		80	960			
Christmas		170	2040			
			0			
			0			
			0			
			0			
Short-term Savings			0			
			0			
Investments			0			
			0			
			0			
			0			
Total discretionary expenses		1595	19140			

* For additional payments above the monthly regular payments.

Illustration 3.4   Form 3.4 with Sample Data

Expenses: Irregular/Predictable (To Be Escrowed) (Form 3.5)

Irregular expenses include those that are predictable but occur at intervals other than regular monthly. Such expenses are frequently large and are budget busters. Property taxes, additional income taxes, insurance premiums (car insurance, home insurance, etc.), school tuition, car repairs, and emergencies fit this category.

If you do not have an emergency fund, it is time to consider creating one. Money in the bank for unexpected expenses equals peace of mind and is the first line of defense for avoiding increasing credit card debt.

Illustration 3.5 shows Form 3.5 with sample data. Blank Form 3.5 appears at the end of this chapter.

Form 3.5   Expenses: Irregular/Predictable (To Be Escrowed)

Item	When due	History Total Amount	History Monthly set aside	Forecast Total Amount	Forecast Monthly set aside *
Taxes					
Property Taxes		2100			
Household					
Automotive					
Insurance					
Homeowners		400			
Vacation/leisure					
Vacation Trip		4500			
Ball Games		1200			
Other					
Emergency fund					
	Totals	8200			

* Assume 1/12th of total

Illustration 3.5   Form 3.5 with Sample Data

Summary of Interest and Fees Paid (Form 3.6)

Interest is a charge paid for the use of someone else's money. Interest increases the cost of anything you buy on credit. When analyzing your bills that include interest, record the interest on the appropriate expense form and also record the interest charges separately on Form 3.6. This form is an

Form 3.6   Summary of Interest and Fees Paid

Loan and purpose	Date	Amount	
		Monthly	Annual
Home mortgage (interest portion)			
Home equity loan or line of credit			
Credit cards (fees and interest)			
Monthly Bank charges/penalties			
Other			
Total Interest Paid			

Illustration 3.6   Sample of Blank Form 3.6

extract of interest information from other forms and sources. Its purpose is to highlight how much money that could be yours is now going to someone else. If you want a raise, the first strategy to generate one is to stop sending your money to someone else.

Illustration 3.6 shows Form 3.6, and another blank of Form 3.6 appears at the end of this chapter.

Sources and Uses of Funds Summary (Form 3.7)

Form 3.7 summarizes funds coming in (sources of money) and funds going out (expenses, or uses of funds). It is a quick check to see if you have covered everything in your history analysis. (Illustration 3.7 shows Form 3.7 with sample data.)

You cannot spend more than you have somehow found funds for, so *"sources of funds" must always equal "uses of funds."*

It is relatively easy to identify all sources of funds. Chances are you cannot as easily account for how the funds were used. That is, you can see from your data that you must have spent the money but do not know how you spent it. So ask yourself this question: If you cannot remember what you spent all that money for, how important was it to spend that money? Answering this question will enable you to begin finding the money you are going to use to give to yourself a raise. Odds are that "unremembered" spent money is the source of some of the leaks in your money bucket. (The section below, "The One-Month Analysis," will help you fill in your memory gaps.)

Your objective in this exercise is to identify where you are getting money and where it is going. The point is not to make value judgments about what you spend money for. The purpose is to give you a very clear picture of your spending habits to allow you to ask the critical question, "Is this how I want to spend my money, or are there better choices I can make?"

Using blank Form 3.7 (found at the end of this chapter), add up your total sources of funds and uses of funds for the year (from Forms 3.1–3.5).

What Form 3.7 Can Tell You

First of all, you must balance the *sources of funds* with the *uses of funds,* since by definition they have to be equal.

If you are short on the sources, chances are you have overlooked either the liquidation of some assets such as savings withdrawals or investment sales, or perhaps your debt increase is greater than you have accounted for.

Form 3.7   Sources and Uses of Funds Summary

Use Annual Figures				
	History	Percent	Forecast	Percent
SOURCES of FUNDS (from Form 3.1)				
Total Current Income	72000			
Total Investment Income				
Total Sale of Assets				
Total Windfalls				
Total Debt Increase	3000			
Total Sources of Funds	75000			
USES of FUNDS				
Monthly FIXED Expenses (from Form 3.2)	28800			
Monthly VARIABLE Expenses (from Form 3.3)	19000			
DISCRETIONARY Expenses (from Form 3.4)	19000			
ESCROWED Expenses (from Form 3.5)	8200			
Total Uses of Funds	75000			
Note: Some figures have been rounded from detailed illustrations				

Illustration 3.7   Sample of Form 3.7 with Sample Data

If your "uses of funds" amount is less than your sources, likely overlooked items might be debt reduction, increased investments and savings, or vacation and recreation items. These items are all discretionary.

In any event, time spent getting the sources and uses of funds aligned will make the entire planning process more rewarding.

The next thing to do is review the sources of funds. Two of the key financial risk assessment elements are income stability and emergency cash reserves. Have you been able to live within your total current income? Selling off assets or increasing debt are not good long-term strategies for safety.

Think now about how you would like to change sources of funds in the future.

You may wish to do further analysis of uses of funds, particularly if you have decided on something like the Jenkins 60 percent plan. Calculate the percentage of funds going into discretionary spending, which includes savings and investing. Is too much of your funding going into fixed expenses, which leaves you with fewer choices (and more risk in tough economic times)?

The Financial Freedom Risk Assessment scale provides a good guideline for how much of your spending should be consumed by routine living expenses. Form 3.7 gives you a rough summary of those areas where you are already committed to spend.

Finally, this form is an excellent estimator of your fit to the Jenkins 60 percent scale. According to the Jenkins plan, you should live on 60 percent of your income, which means the total of monthly fixed expenses and monthly variable expenses should be 60 percent. Discretionary spending should be 30 percent—to cover 10 percent for investing, 10 percent for savings, and 10 percent for fun. The last 10 percent should cover escrow for irregular major expenses.

Start thinking about what you need to change to fit your plan.

The One-Month Analysis: A Supplement to Your Data

As mentioned above, you may have realized that you just do not know where you are spending your money. If you are unable to identify or categorize nearly all of your spending from your records, you will need to supplement your data by doing the following one-month analysis (alternatively, the one-month approach can be used to replace the records-based analysis—more about that below).

Spending money is something to which we pay little attention, particularly if things are going well. If asked to list from memory the money you spent over the last week, it is unlikely that you will recall more than 50 percent of your expenditures with any degree of accuracy. To remedy this deficiency, consider undertaking the following.

In addition to the rather lengthy process of assembling your history from last year's records, you may want to track one month's income and spending in fine detail. Keep track of all "money in" for one month and keep track of everything you spend for one month. EVERYTHING! Then categorize the spending and record it. Use the same categories that you used in gathering your data, and for consistency, you may want to make a duplicate set of Forms 3.1 through 3.7 and record the monthly figures on those duplicate forms (for most annual columns, multiply one month's spending by 12).

Of course, monthly fixed expenses are relatively easy to gather from your one-month analysis (for annual total, simply multiply one month's expenses by 12), but you probably will confirm that you already identified them in your previous record sorting. But this one-month exercise is especially useful in obtaining a more accurate picture of the elusive monthly variable and discretionary expenses (again, for an annual total, multiply most one-month figures by 12). On the downside, this exercise does not yield a complete picture of all annual expenses because it does not take into consideration expenses that do not predictably occur every month. However, it is an excellent exercise to help decide a realistic amount to allot to personal allowances and variable and discretionary expenses.

Again, the purpose of this one-month trial is not to judge the wisdom of the spending, but rather for you to become aware of leaks in the money bucket to which you have become insensitive.

How to Analyze a Month of Your Spending

The three major sources of information about monthly spending are:

1. Your bank statement (and/or checkbook register)

2. Your credit card statement/s

3. Receipts for everything

Bank statements and credit card statements are rarely cycled to the exact calendar month, so you may need two of them to track a particular calendar month.

The aim is to analyze one month's spending information by category in a manner consistent with your records analysis. If you completed the Chapter 3 forms (Forms 3.1–3.7) or created your own forms, just be sure to record the one-month data on the same forms and divide it into the same categories.

Your task is for one month to amass all receipts, credit card statements, and check registers; analyze them; and categorize your spending. Two words of caution: (1) Be careful to avoid counting an expense twice (for example, a receipt for items *charged* on your credit card at Target should not be counted again when you categorize the credit card statement on which that same charge appears); and (2) many receipts/charges contain items in multiple categories.

Receipts

Nearly every purchase has a receipt, whether you pay cash for a candy bar and magazine or charge a shopping spree at Wal-Mart. For one month, keep every receipt. Most charges give you the option for getting a receipt. Get one whenever you can. At the end of the day, on each receipt note what it was for and put it in a box or envelope. Write clearly to jog your memory, because at the end of the month, without clear annotations some of the receipts will perplex you and you will not remember what they were for.

For those rare instances when you do not receive a receipt, keep a small notepad to write down what you spend. Tips for personal service, vending machine purchases, and church offerings come to mind as "receipt-less" transactions.

When you are trying to analyze where your money goes by category (such as groceries, automotive, etc.), some receipts contain items in just one category, like a gasoline receipt, but many receipts contain items in numerous categories. For example, at discount stores, a single receipt may reflect purchases in many categories: two DVDs (recreation), apples and hamburger (groceries), linens and household items (household supplies), aspirin (medical), sweater (clothing), and card table (furniture).

Illustrations 3.8, 3.9, 3.10, and 3.11 are sample statements and receipts and are intended to illustrate the process of annotating and categorizing receipts/statements. They are included to point out the possible complexity of gathering historical data from multiple sources and to clarify the need to isolate different kinds of expenses. The "callout categories" used in the illustrations are not intended to be categories for you. Rather, the markups are meant to illustrate that clarity is what you need when you analyze where your money is being spent. Even if lawn mower repairs and groceries show up on the same charge card statement, they are clearly different and need to be separated into different categories that make sense to you.

At first glance the Costco receipt (Illustration 3.8) seems to be for groceries, but it would be a distortion if you categorized the total receipt as "groceries" for the month. In fact, 39 percent of the expenses are for nongrocery items: Laundry detergent and trash bags are "laundry/cleaning supplies," one item was a "gift," vitamins and pain pills are "medical" expenses.

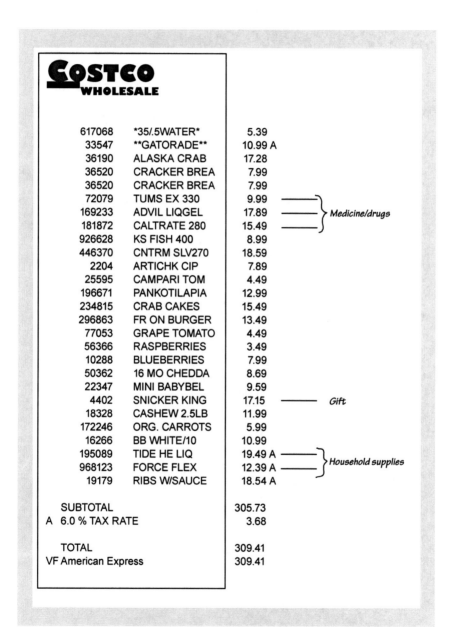

Illustration 3.8   Annotated Costco Receipt

The Acme receipt (Illustration 3.9) tells a similarly mixed tale. Of the total bill, 37 percent are nongrocery items: Toilet cleaner, carpet cleaner, toothpaste, and a measuring cup are all household supplies.

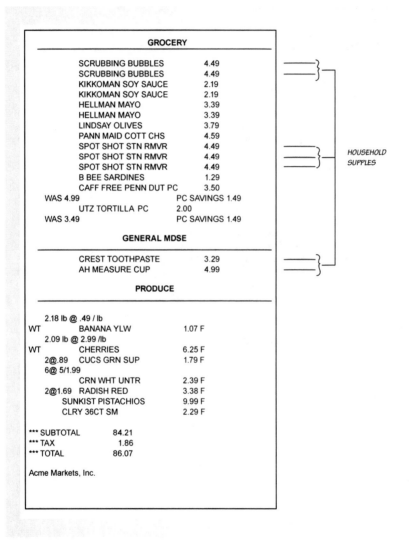

Illustration 3.9   Annotated Acme Receipt

Credit Card Statements

Most of your monthly credit card statements will include purchases in multiple categories, so you'll need to annotate each statement. Also, for any charge on the statement for which you have a receipt, cross the charge off the card and capture the purchase from the receipt instead. That is, take care to count each expense only once: Either count the receipt or count the charge on the credit card statement, but not both.

The credit card statement excerpted below (Illustration 3.10) shows both the usefulness of the statement for some categories and the need for backup receipts for charges such as Costco. Until you sort out the categories, you do not have much useful information.

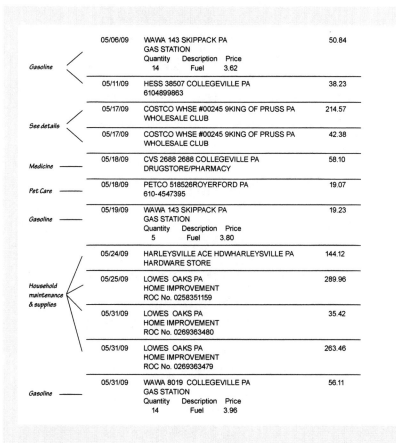

Illustration 3.10   Annotated Credit Card Statement Excerpt

Bank Statements

The sample bank statement in Illustration 3.11 is much like the credit card statement. You have to be careful that you do not count something twice. If you have a receipt for something that you paid for by check and then itemize it for this exercise, be sure when you look at your check register not to include the same items twice in your analysis.

	Amount	Transactions	
Subscription	14.79-	The Inquirer	Bill Payment
Personal Care	32.00-	Kihm's Sonny 130 W. Main St	04/29 #000490700 Purchase Trappe PA
	67.62+	Deposit	
Utility	35.00-	Skippack Township Sewer Fund Bill Payment	
Clothing	230.02-	Nordstrom 629 190 North Gulph R King Of Prus PA	05/03 #000546354 Purchase
Home Repairs	40.86-	Lowe's #1047 200-B Mill Rd Pob Oaks PA	05/03 #000546354 Purchase
Groceries	20.66-	Acme 222 West Main St. Collegeville PA	05/02 #000747999 Purchase
Medicine	11.67-	Cvs 2350 Bridge Road & Ski Skippack PA	05/03 #000126261 Purchase
	10.47-	Cvs 2688 55 Park Ave	05/03 #000052912 Purchase Collegeville PA
Personal Care	86.52-	CheckCard 0503 Skippack PA 246326981261	Salon Rouge Inc.
Church	142.68-	Check 2568	
Pet Care	97.41-	CheckCard 0506 Yoshiko'S Skippack PA 240726981803	
See details	2,500.00+	Deposit	
	168.80-	Costco Whse #0 15255 N. Hayden R Scottsdale AZ	05/09 #0000000278 Purchase
Pet Care	62.00-	Charlene's Pet Sitting Service Bill Payment	
Insurance	281.67-	Travelers Insur	Des:Insurance IDxxxxx0920 Co ID:9130245801
Utility	174.25-	Peco Energy	Bill Payment
Medicine	64.68-	CheckCard 0510 Miles Pharmacy 610-287-6446 PA 254568964345677	
Groceries	60.93-	Albertsons 11475 E. Via Lind Scottsdale AZ	05/09 #00094574325 Purchase

Illustration 3.11   Annotated Check Register/Bank Statement

Because we have so many diverse ways to spend money, it is very easy to become oblivious to what is going where. Our addiction to credit cards makes the problem worse. Remember again, this analysis is not about value judgments. It is about looking at money that currently you are spending mindlessly, becoming aware of how you are spending the money, and replacing your unthinking habit with purposeful spending. Self-control is hard if you do not know what you need to control.

One-Month Analysis: A Last Resort for the Recordless

As mentioned briefly above, it is possible to do only the one-month analysis; that is, to do the one-month exercise *instead of* the more thorough records-based analysis. If you have no records or your records are very incomplete, you may want to use this approach. It isn't nearly as accurate a record of income and spending, but it's better than nothing.

To rely entirely on the one-month analysis, do the following:

1. Follow the guidelines above about recording all income and spending for one month and analyze it and record it as directed. It's fine to use the forms from Chapter 3 for this purpose.

2. Since no one month captures predictable expenses that occur at irregular intervals, you will need to compile a list of your expenses that are irregular (like auto insurance) and record the costs. If you cannot reconstruct these expenses by estimating, contact the companies you pay to find out the amounts of your "predictable but irregular" bills.

Summary

Congratulations! If you've filled out the forms in this chapter, you have done the most time-consuming part of your job. The "history" data you've gathered show how you got where you are today. Carved on the National Archives Building in Washington, D.C., is "What's Past Is Prologue," taken from Shakespeare's play, *The Tempest*. Our past is the foundation for the future and helps point the way.

The sample forms also have forecast (or future) columns. Set the forms aside for now and we will come back to them later in Chapter 5. Very soon it will be time to do the "fun" part of all this records gathering—figuring out where the leaks are in your money bucket and planning how to plug the leaks and give yourself that raise!

Chapter 1 provided a quick assessment of your financial health, and Chapter 3 has provided a framework for gathering a history of your money to show you how you got where you are today. In Chapter 4, "Setting Goals," I will explore why it is vital to think through what you really want to accomplish. In Chapter 5, I'll cover how to integrate your goals with a financial plan based on your spending patterns.

≫ *Being Part of the Money* ≪
Management Process:
A Special Benefit for Women

While I was reviewing this chapter with a widow friend, she asked if I was planning any special section for women and their absolute need to participate in the family finances. I had not, but the lesson she learned needs to be shared.

Her story is an interesting one. She and her late husband were financially secure, and perhaps what most would consider well off. They each had enough money to indulge themselves, but typically major purchases were discussed in advance so there would be no surprises or conflict.

Since he was an entrepreneur type and enjoyed controlling things and people, it was left to him to manage the family finances. As he aged and fell into poor health, she let him continue to manage the money part of their lives to, as she put it, "please him."

As his health deteriorated more and his attentiveness and judgment also worsened, she began seeing alarming nonpayment notices and threats of collection action. Rather than intrude on his domain, she merely contacted the various companies and had the bills set up for automatic payment.

This strategy, she concluded, was far better than confrontation or taking away something he valued doing. This was a loving decision but, as it turned out, a very wrong one.

Only a few months after he died, she received a shocking letter from the U.S. Internal Revenue Service—the dreaded IRS—announcing their intent to seize all of her assets to cover tens of thousands of dollars of tax assessments and penalties due immediately. Her late husband had simply stopped filing tax returns.

On reflection, she realized that letting him continue his sole control of their finances was misplaced love and loyalty. It nearly destroyed her and could have been easily avoided if they had openly shared the process.

In a marriage, both parties need to be participants in the financial elements of their life together. Anything less is irresponsible and immature.

Form 3.1   Sources of Funds

Item	History			Forecast		
	When received	Amount		When received	Amount	
		Monthly	Annual		Monthly	Annual
CURRENT INCOME						
Wages/Salary: Gross pay						
Payroll deductions are listed on Form 3-2 as regular monthly fixed expenses.						
Commissions						
Overtime						
Bonuses						
Part-time income						
Other						
Total Current Income						
INVESTMENTS						
Interest Received						
Dividends						
Annuities						
Pension or retirement payout						
Social Security						
Other						
Total Investment Income						
ASSET SALE/Redemption						
Stock/bond sale proceeds						
Savings Withdrawal						
CDs maturing						
Sale of other assets						
Total Asset Proceeds						
WINDFALLS						
Tax refund						
Gifts/Inheritances						
Other (specify)						
Total Windfall						
DEBT INCREASE						
Credit card, increased balance						
Home equity loan or credit line						
Refinance home						
Personal loans						
Installment purchases						
Borrowing from retirement funds						
Other						
Total Debt Increase						
Total Source of Funds						

Form 3.2   Expenses: Regular Monthly Fixed Amounts

Item	When Paid	History		Forecast	
		Monthly	Annually	Monthly	Annually
Payroll Deductions					
Federal income tax					
State income tax					
Local income tax					
Social Security					
Retirement contribution (401k)					
Insurance					
Loan payments					
Other					
Mortgage/Rent					
Automobile Loan(s)					
Other Loans					
Other					
Total Current Regular Fixed Expenses					

Note: The full payments for loans should be entered on this form. Wherever possible to identify
the interest amount enter that on form 3.6 as well.

Form 3.3   Expenses: Regular Monthly Variable Amounts

Item	When paid	History Amount			Forecast Amount	
		Monthly	Annually	Average/mo	Monthly	Annually
Utilities						
Electrical						
Gas/Oil						
Water						
Sewer						
Trash pick-up						
Cable						
Telephone (s)						
Food/Groceries						
Transportation						
Automotive						
Fuel						
Parking/tolls						
Credit card interest *						
Bank charges						
Other						
Total Variable Monthly Expenses						

* Also enter the interest paid on form 3.6

Form 3.4   Expenses: Discretionary

Item	Who pays	History Amount Monthly	History Amount Annual	History Average/mo	Forecast Amount Monthly	Forecast Amount Annual
Personal Items						
Allowances						
Medical/Dental						
Recreation/Entertainment						
Debt reduction *						
Other						
Short-term Savings						
Investments						
Total discretionary expenses						

* For additional payments above the monthly regular payments.

Form 3.5   Expenses: Irregular/Predictable (To Be Escrowed)

Item	History			Forecast	
	When due	Total Amount	Monthly set aside	Total Amount	Monthly set-aside *
Taxes					
Household					
Automotive					
Insurance					
Vacation/leisure					
Other					
Emergency fund					
Totals					

* Assume 1/12th of total

Form 3.6   Summary of Interest and Fees Paid

Loan and purpose	Date	Amount	
		Monthly	Annual
Home mortgage (interest portion)			
Home equity loan or line of credit			
Credit cards (fees and interest)			
Monthly Bank charges/penalties			
Other			
Total Interest Paid			

Form 3.7   Sources and Uses of Funds Summary

Use Annual Figures				
	History	Percent	Forecast	Percent
SOURCES of FUNDS (from Form 3.1)				
Total Current Income				
Total Investment Income				
Total Sale of Assets				
Total Windfalls				
Total Debt Increase				
Total Sources of Funds				
USES of FUNDS				
Monthly FIXED Expenses (from Form 3.2)				
Monthly VARIABLE Expenses (from Form 3.3)				
DISCRETIONARY Expenses (from Form 3.4)				
ESCROWED Expenses (from Form 3.5)				
Total Uses of Funds				

CHAPTER FOUR

Setting Goals

After taking the Risk Assessment quiz in Chapter 1, you have an idea of your financial risk and your financial health. After analyzing your financial history in Chapter 3, you know the details of your own financial "bucket." Now you are in a position to thoughtfully set personal goals to guide your financial future.

Getting in over Your Head

The past 20 to 30 years have witnessed a significant cultural shift toward instant gratification and away from plan, save, and only then buy. Instant and virtually unlimited access to credit has made delaying gratification something a lot of people have never had to do. Report after report laments that personal savings rates are at an all-time low, and at the same time, consumer debt is at an all-time high and growing.

If you are living beyond your means and are getting deeper in debt, the illusion is that all your troubles would be solved if only you had more money coming in. The unfortunate truth is that most people ramp up their spending as fast or faster than the dollar amount of their raises. We tend to live in anticipation of a better future, and we spend as if tomorrow were already here.

The long-term solution to this pattern is to take control of your money life, live within your present means, get out of debt and stay out of debt, save for the rainy day, and—this is the key—be happy and content with what you have. A buying spree as a remedy for discontent or depression (some call it "retail therapy") can become chronic self-destructive behavior. You have better choices.

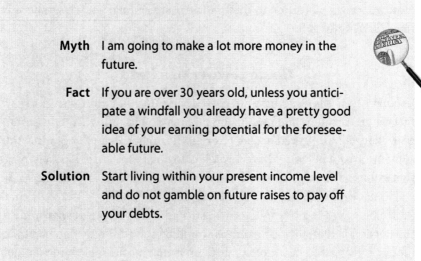

Myth   Money problems are self-correcting.

Fact   Left alone, problems usually get worse. Thinking otherwise is self-delusion.

Solution   Commit to taking active charge of your money life.

Myth   I am going to make a lot more money in the future.

Fact   If you are over 30 years old, unless you anticipate a windfall you already have a pretty good idea of your earning potential for the foreseeable future.

Solution   Start living within your present income level and do not gamble on future raises to pay off your debts.

Why You Need Written Goals

Chances are that you can identify a substantial amount of cash that is being wasted within your present income. This "found cash" is exactly like a raise you give yourself because you can do the same things with it that you can do with a raise.

The first step toward spending control is to write down what you want your income to do for you (your goals) and then resist or avoid doing things that do not help you reach your goals.

Our financial lives need goals. Goals organize our activities, control our behavior, and provide focus, and goals are a way to define success. Goals help us select priorities. Goals are a way to deflect random impulse spending that does not help us reach our objectives. Unless you write down your goals and commit to reaching them, they are simply dreams.

The No-Goal Life

A cynic once observed, "Money does not buy you happiness, but it sure pays for a lot of things that make you forget you are unhappy." Are you using retail therapy (buying binges) to cover up some underlying discontent? Are you in debt because of it?

Look around and ask yourself what you have acquired that truly makes you happy. Are there a lot of things that, now that you have them, somehow are less satisfying than you expected? And how do you explain that feeling? "It seemed like a good idea at the time" reflects the insight that perhaps given the opportunity to decide again, you might do things differently.

Goal setting is a process to get rid of that regretful hindsight: "If I had only known then what I know now, maybe . . ."

The Goal-Setting Process

"If you do not know where you are going, any place gets you there."

We have all heard this expression and know what it means. Anytime we plan a vacation, we start with a destination in mind. When we tell our friends we are going on a vacation, their first question is, "Where are you going?" And rarely is our answer, "Oh, just any place we happen to end up." Yet we do that very thing with our financial life, which, when you think about it, is pretty silly.

Goal setting is a six-step process of answering these questions:

1. What do I want?

2. How much will it cost?

3. How much time will it take?

4. When do I want to reach the goal?

5. What steps do I have to take to get what I want?

6. How will I know that I have reached the goal?

Limitations of time and money are important factors in the process. Money spent for Goal A is not available for Goal B; priorities need to be established. We all have exactly the same amount of time, and time spent working on Goal A is not available for working on Goal B.

It is important to be specific about the answers to the six preceding questions. For example, if one of your goals is to "be happy," how will you know when you have achieved that goal? You need to specify the components of happiness.

You could do almost *anything* you want in life, but it is unlikely that you can do *everything* you want to do. Choices are inevitable; make them deliberately and not by accident.

Who Should Set Goals?

Goal setting is relatively simple when you are only dealing with yourself. Add other significant people to your life, and the choices grow exponentially. Priorities for the use of money will be different, but so will priorities for the use of time. For example, whose family will we visit on the holidays? Where and when do we go on vacation? Which restaurant are we going to Friday night? You can add literally hundreds of such dilemmas. Without goals and a system for prioritizing them, stress is inevitable.

Begin with setting individual personal goals. Then, if you are part of a family situation, meet as a group to begin a negotiating process on group goals. Some goals will be common and agreed upon, and some will be in conflict. Ultimately, individual goals and group goals must live in harmony. Ignoring this process almost guarantees conflict and strife where there should be accord and cooperation.

Personal Goals

Personal goals can be grouped into three categories:

1. **Stuff:** things I want to acquire.

2. **Experiences:** activities I want to do.

3. **Wealth building:** getting out of debt and financial assets and wealth I want accumulate.

Use the following three forms to record your goals.

- Form 4.1: Things I Want to Acquire

- Form 4.2: Experiences I Want to Have

- Form 4.3: Assets and Wealth I Want to Accumulate

Illustrations 4.1, 4.2, and 4.3 show these forms with sample data. Blanks of the forms appear at the end of this chapter. (Or make up your own simple forms. Full-size forms that can be downloaded and personalized are available on our Web site: www.ptff.net.) For each category, include small and short-term goals as well as the more grandiose wishes that will take longer to achieve.

Form 4.1   Things I Want to Acquire

Name		Date	
Rank	What	When	$ Cost
	New/Used Car for Sue	2 years from now	$ 18,000
	Addition to House	3 years from now	$ 40,000
	Used Car for John	4 years from now	$ 12,000
	Piano	3 years from now	$ 10,000

Illustration 4.1   Form 4.1 with Sample Data

Form 4.2   Experiences I Want to Have

Rank	What	When	$ Cost	Time Req.
	Trip to visit Joe's family	3 years	$ 5,000	2 weeks
	Caribbean Cruise for Joe and Sue's Anniversary	7 years	$ 6,000	10 days
	Visit Baseball Hall of Fame	2 years	$ 4,000	1 week

Name _____   Date _____

Illustration 4.2   Form 4.2 with Sample Data

Form 4.3   Assets and Wealth I Want to Accumulate

Name _____   Date _____

Rank	What	When	Amount
	College for John	4 years	$ 40,000
	College for Shelley	8 years	$ 40,000
	Retirement	20 years	?
	Emergency Fund	1 year	$ 10,000

Illustration 4.3   Form 4.3 with Sample Data

Remember, there are no right answers. The whole purpose of this exercise is to give you personal control of how you spend to get the most satisfaction from your money. Purposeful spending is always more satisfying over the long term than impulse buying. If you do not think out your goals in advance, every new thing becomes tempting and impulse buying is the result.

Make sure that all of your goals are realistic. It is up to you to decide how you will adjust your other spending to achieve them. After you have "dreamed" and listed everything you can think of, order your list by priority (highest to lowest).

Finally, make a list of the 10 top priorities right now, combining "Things," "Experiences," and "Assets and Wealth." This exercise is the beginning of controlling your impulse spending and is discussed further in Chapter 8, Spending Strategies. A very large portion of your budget is allocated for routine and predictable purposes. The risk comes when our "gotta have that" impulses are triggered by the lure of something nice and well merchandised that enters our life.

Whether it be sales pressure or peer pressure or the simple emotional desire to have something, we need to have a rational way to stay in control. By deciding in advance what our priorities are, we can ask ourselves before the impulse purchase why we should spend on something not already on the list.

As you will learn, everyone needs some totally discretionary money on a daily basis (an allowance of sorts). But if a contemplated purchase is not in the plan and cannot be purchased out of your current allowance, it should be put in the plan to substitute for something already there. That is, if you are sure you want to spend money on something not on the list, revise the list and replace it with your new most-important-thing-to-spend-money-on.

For example, let's imagine that you are into photography and see the latest expensive revolutionary lens at a display in the shopping mall, which costs a mere $750 (plus tax). If you spend the money for this, something else must come off your goal list. Having goals makes you think things through to avoid impulse purchases.

The Family Process

Once your individual goals are listed and prioritized, it is time to meet as a family. Obviously, there will be individual goals and family goals, and they will likely compete for the same money and the same time.

Enjoy the process of reviewing every family member's goals and work toward building a comprehensive plan. There will be give and take, and in the end you should try to develop a master list that includes everyone.

Goals as a Spending Strategy

Part of the problem we all face is that we have endless appetites for something new. Spending money is fun, but being in debt is not. With an agreed goal list, your day-to-day temptation for spending is more restrained and focused. Impulses are more easily controlled.

A core premise of this book is that debt is not a good thing. So being debt free should be high on the goal list. As debt goes away, more money is available for current choices. The interest and finance charges you avoid when out of debt are a real raise for you.

Postponing gratification is a matter of personal discipline. The wrong choice is to give in to the desire for something "right now" by borrowing or going into debt to attain it.

Revising Goals

You need to revise your goals any time significant changes occur. In fact, it would be a good idea to conduct an annual review to measure progress, add new goals, shift priorities, and drop goals that no longer seem important.

Myth   Tomorrow will take care of itself. Something
good will happen, so why worry about it now?

Fact   Tomorrow *will* take care of itself, but will it take
care of you? Don't plan on it. You need to take
care of you. Faith has limits, as the following
story illustrates.

*The river flood came quickly and severely, and
farmer Ralph climbed up on the porch roof.
When offered a ride off by the sheriff's boat,
Ralph declined and said he had faith in the Lord.
Hours later a second boat came by, and again
he declined to be rescued and professed his faith.
Finally near dusk the river had risen further, so
Ralph was on the top ridge of the roof when a heli-
copter offered to pick him up. Again he declined.*

*In the night he was swept off by the rising waters
and went to meet the Lord. "I had faith, Lord," he
said. "Why did you let me down?" To which the
Lord replied, "I sent two boats and a helicopter—
what more did you expect?"*

Solution   Help is everywhere if you will only take advantage of it. Take charge of your money life by rec-
ognizing you need to be in control and that you
can be in control.

>> *Can You Really Save 10 Percent?* <<

The first rule from *The Richest Man in Babylon* (Clason) is "pay yourself first." "Easier said than done," you may say. After all, you are running out of money before the end of the month, so how could you get by on less?

Your mind set has to change. You have to pay yourself first instead of last. You cannot wait to pay yourself last hoping there will be something left over, which there never is. You worked to earn it. Keep some of your money for the inevitable "rainy day" or retirement or whatever you choose to call tomorrow.

Research has proven it is harder to spend cash than to use a credit card, because using cash gives a more personal feeling of giving up something valuable. It is also harder to spend a big bill than a small bill.

Try this experiment. Take $100, or some other sum of money that you would expect to cover your pocket money for one week. Have the money sorted into five $1 bills, one $5 bill, two $10 bills, one $20 bill, and one $50 bill.

First, take one of the $10 bills and put it aside where you cannot get to it easily. Forget the $10 bill. If self-control is a real issue when it comes to spending, make getting to the $10 nearly impossible. Maybe put it in a food storage bag and put the bag in an empty milk container, fill it with water, and put it in the freezer. It will require real determination to spend that $10.

Now your challenge is to get through the week with the $90 cash you have. Spend your cash however you want. Do not go to the trouble of making a written budget in advance. Just be aware that the $90 is all you have to spend. At the end of the week, reflect on how you managed the cash you had.

You did not start out with a written budget. You merely started out with a set amount of cash and the knowledge that it had to last. As each spending opportunity presented itself, you undoubtedly paused to be certain that spending some of your money was a wise and timely decision. If you made it through the week, you proved you can easily save 10 percent simply by "paying yourself first!"

It is time to continue the habit.

Form 4.1   Things I Want to Acquire

Name _____   Date _____

Rank	What	When	$ Cost

Form 4.2   Experiences I Want to Have

Name _____		Date _____		
Rank	What	When	$ Cost	Time Req.

Form 4.3   Assets and Wealth I Want to Accumulate

Name			Date
Rank	What	When	Amount

CHAPTER FIVE

More About Forecasting

If you are using this book as a financial planning blueprint, you have by now assessed your financial freedom risk and decided on a broad plan for what needs changing (Chapters 1 and 2), painstakingly gathered and categorized the details of last year's flow of funds (Chapter 3), and reflected on your future goals (Chapter 4).

In this chapter, you will refine all of this information into a specific financial plan. Then, in Chapter 6, I will show you a powerful system for implementing your plan and seamlessly managing your money by relying on the power of modern electronic banking: the Freedom Money Management System™.

An Iterative Process

Iterative may not be a word familiar to you, but it is the right term to describe the forecasting process. It is a fancy way to say "repetitive," "trial and error," or "give and take." A single forecasting effort will probably not be enough for you to rearrange your priorities and face the reality that there never seems to be enough money coming in to do everything. Several iterations may be required, and each trial forecast (or iteration) should get you closer to a workable plan. It is somewhat like focusing binoculars—you zoom in and out until things are sharp and in focus.

The forecasting process is the same no matter where you are starting. The details will be different for everyone because only you can decide what is right for you. In this chapter, I will give you a few tips or suggestions on how to do your forecast.

Getting control of your finances may be easy or difficult depending on your individual circumstances. However, the harder it is, the more likely you are already in pretty bad shape, which means that the ultimate benefits to you will be very significant.

Using History Forms for Forecasting

The history forms you completed in Chapter 3 contain the details of your own real spending and are central to the forecasting process (Forms 3.1–3.5).

For every entry on those forms there was a forecast column. To focus on how you want to change past spending habits, take each form and go over it line by line, asking yourself the following questions about each line:

- Do I want to change this?

- Why do I want to change it?

- How do I want to or need to change this?

- Can I change this? If not, why can't I?

- What would need to happen to enable me to make the changes I want?

- What is the benefit of changing the item or category?

- What is the disadvantage of not changing it?

- When can I change it?

- If I decide to change the item, what is the new forecast dollar amount?

Anything can be changed in the future if you have enough motivation and time. Obviously some things are dramatically life-changing, such as deciding that your house is too big or too expensive and that to survive and thrive you need to sell it. Other things, like cutting back on recreational expenses for a while, are easier to accomplish.

We all wish that changes could be painless, and maybe you only need to make some modifications to an otherwise wholesome financial situation. If so, that is an easy call and you can begin right away. But what about the tough decisions? When you get the wake-up call that there is no way your income and projected income can sustain your present life style, how long can you put off taking the first step to change things? Putting off the inevitable usually makes things worse later. Reality is sometimes cruel, but once you face it and deal with it, you will begin a better life. I hope that this book will motivate you and show you the way to deal with the issues.

Issues to Deal With

Here are my recommendations in a few typical areas that inevitably generate questions during the forecasting process.

Pay Yourself First

The basic rule from all financial advisors and experts is: Pay yourself the first 10 percent of everything you earn. This 10 percent savings should be the first line on your spending plan (and you should include it with the Form 3.2 forecasts and also on Form 5.1 or Form 5.1a, discussed below). If your employer offers a 401(k) or similar plan, sign up to have the 10 percent taken from your paycheck automatically. If your employer matches your savings up to a certain level, be sure to participate up to the maximum the employer allows.

This money is money you should forget about for a long time. Ask older friends if they wish they had started saving 20 years ago. Time flies, and the power of compound interest works more dramatically the longer the savings are held.

Stop Increasing Your Debt

Before you can begin to get out of debt, you must stop getting deeper into debt. The logical first step is to stop paying by credit. That's fundamental. But if you stop paying by credit, how will you pay? Small items can be paid for in cash, but what about big items that you've always charged?

Escrowing is the first step to stopping growing debt. You need to immediately *begin escrowing funds* for such major expenses *so in the future you can avoid paying for these expenses by credit.*

I am a firm believer in escrowing—that is, regularly setting aside money to accumulate to pay for big expenses that will be coming up at irregular intervals throughout the year. An example of escrow presents itself in many home mortgages. If you purchased your home with less than 20 percent down, the lender will typically require an escrow account to pay for taxes and insurance when they are due. Each month an amount equal to one-twelfth of the estimated amount for taxes and insurance will be added to your mortgage payment. The mortgage company *escrows* this "extra" money and uses it to pay the property tax and insurance bills when they come due.

In terms of your spending plan, therefore, your next priority after "paying yourself first" is to set aside money in an *escrow account* to be prepared for predictable big items that you know will be coming up (record the escrow forecasts on Form 3.5 and on Form 5.1 or Form 5.1a). Discretionary expenses like vacations need to be accumulated for in this same way (forecasts for such expenses should be recorded on Form 3.4 and on Form 5.1 or Form 5.1a). If you cannot accumulate the funds in advance, do not incur the expenses.

In your forecast calculations, also add an extra $100 a month to start an emergency fund (record this forecast on Form 3.5). Something *unexpected* can be *expected* to happen when it is most inconvenient for you.

Get out of Debt

After you have set aside money to keep your debt from growing in the future, you need to have a plan to get out of debt forever. Chapter 7 describes the technique for debt management. In that chapter, you will see how to estimate how fast you can get out of debt and how much effort that will take.

If, for example, over the past two years you have used your credit cards to supplement your income and you now have an unpaid balance of $6,000 (which is unfortunately typical), you have dug the debt hole deeper by an average of $250 a month ($6,000 debt/24 months = $250 per month).

Just to stop "digging the hole," you will need to find $250 in your monthly expenses that you are able to stop spending. And if you want to get out of debt (pay off the $6,000 unpaid credit card balances) in the next two years, which is the same period of time it took you to get this far behind, you are going to have to find at least an additional $250 a month to put toward that purpose.

In this example, getting out of debt means you have to trim your expenses

$500 a month on your forecasts (look at the expenses on Forms 3.2 through 3.5 to identify categories where you can forecast reduced expenses; then once you've decided where to cut, also record the summary forecast on Form 5.1 or Form 5.1a). Not only will getting out of debt bring peace of mind, but also you will no longer be paying interest on the debt, and that savings is "found" money—you'll be giving yourself a raise.

Could you use an extra $1,000 next year? If so, get out of debt. The monthly interest at 18 percent (common on credit card balances) on a $6,000 balance is $90. What exactly are you getting for that?

What If I Cannot Both Save and Get out of Debt?

If you cannot both save the ideal minimum amount (for escrow and emergency purposes) and also put aside money for debt reduction, determine the maximum amount you *can* set aside and allocate the money half and half to these two items. This approach is a compromise: while you are getting out of debt, you have to pay savings *and* debt reduction. You need to see that money is growing for the future and that you are getting out of debt, too. Once you are out of debt, you can increase your savings, but it is important to develop a habit of setting aside money immediately.

Another way to look at it is that if you concentrate only on getting out of debt and then find you have to borrow the money right back, you are going to get mighty discouraged. You have to get out of debt while simultaneously setting aside some money to keep from getting back in the same hole.

Sample Forecast

Form 5.1a is a blank worksheet for developing a forecast; if you use it, you'll supply your own expense categories. Form 5.1 is the same form with some suggested categories, and Illustration 5.1 shows Form 5.1 with sample data. Explaining the forecasting process is harder than actually doing it, so an example will serve as a starting point for your own effort. (Blanks of Forms 5.1a and 5.1 appear at the end of the chapter and can be found on our Web site, www.ptff.net.)

Assume the fictional Johnson family from Chapter 3 decides to try the Jenkins 60 percent plan with slight modification. Remember their total family annual income is $72,000. They are planning to allocate their current income to the following six major categories:

- 10 percent   Permanent savings/retirement

- 10 percent   Escrow set-aside for major items

- 60 percent   Day-to-day living expenses (these are fixed monthly, variable monthly, and some of the discretionary categories)

- 10 percent   Fun/leisure/recreation

- 5 percent   Get-out-of-debt allocation

- 5 percent   Savings for goals

Within the day-to-day living expense category, subtotals are set up for fixed monthly, variable monthly, and discretionary expenses to make planning a little more precise and relevant.

Also note that almost everyone has some deductions taken from his or her paycheck, including taxes. When you make your own plan, you need to incorporate those figures in the allocations (Illustration 5.1 and Form 5.1 set up withheld taxes as a subtotal under the day-to-day fixed category).

With this starting point, the following is the annual and monthly allocation of money:

Percent	Category	Annual/Monthly
10 percent	Permanent savings/retirement	$7,200/$600
10 percent	Escrow set-aside for major items	$7,200/$600
60 percent	Day-to-day living expenses	$43,200/$3,600
10 percent	Fun/leisure/recreation	$7,200/$600
5 percent	Get-out-of-debt allocation	$3,600/$300
5 percent	Savings for goals	$3,600/$300

Follow along with Illustration 5.1 (shows Form 5.1 with sample data) as the forecast develops to compare the "Target" (column showing the plan as outlined above), "History" (column showing what the history analysis discloses about what has gone before), and "Change" (column recording what changes will be needed to meet the target plan).

Form 5.1   Forecasting Worksheet

Date _____

Category	Target %	Target Annual $	Target Monthly $	History %	History Annual $	History Monthly $	Change to meet target % (+/-)	Change to meet target Annual $	Change to meet target Monthly $
Permanent savings/retirement	10%	$7,200	$600	2%	$1,080	$90	8%	$6,120	$510
Escrow set aside for major items	10%	$7,200	$600	3%	$2,500		7%	$4,700	$392
Day-to-day living expenses >>total	60%	$43,200	$3,600	78%	$58,980	$4,915	-18%	($15,780)	($1,315)
Sub-totals									
•Fixed	30%	$21,600	$1,800	38%	$27,600	$2,300		($6,000)	($500)
--Taxes withheld					$11,160	$930			$0
--Other items withheld					$2,880	$240			$0
--Other fixed					$13,560	$1,130			$0
•Variable	20%	$14,400	$1,200	17%	$12,420	$1,035		$1,980	$165
•Discretionary	10%	$7,200	$600	26%	$18,960	$1,580		($11,760)	($980)
Fun/leisure/recreation	10%	$7,200	$600	17%	$12,470	$1,040	-7%	($5,270)	($439)
Get-out-of-debt allocation	5%	$3,600	$300	0%	$0	$0	5%	$3,600	$300
Savings for Goals	5%	$3,600	$300	0%	$0	$0	5%	$3,600	$300
TOTALS	100%	$72,000		100%	$75,000			($3,000)	($250)

Note: Shaded areas are sub-totals. Some figures have been rounded for simplicity.

Illustration 5.1   Form 5.1 with Sample Data

The "Target" for permanent savings/retirement is 10 percent, which is the basic amount I mandate in this book as well as the amount suggested by most other experts. However, "History" shows that only $1,080 (or 2 percent) has been set aside for this category. The "Change" needed is another 8 percent , $6,120 annually or $510 per month. It may be that this amount can be withheld from wages paid.

The next category is escrow set-aside, that is, money that is planned to be spent in the future. History for our sample shows that $2,500 (3 percent) was set aside. By setting aside money in anticipation of upcoming bills, day-to-day living expenses may be reduced since there is no need to juggle the bills when the big ones come due. The change required to meet the target in the example is $392 a month.

Skip over the day-to-day category for a moment and look at the last three categories: fun/leisure/recreation; get-out-of-debt allocation; savings for goals. Fun/leisure/recreation was historically higher than the "Target," so a $439-a-month reduction is called for in that category. Nothing was allocated for a debt reduction program or for savings toward goals. Cutting back on recreation will partially offset these; however, another $300 a month will be needed in these two areas.

Now take a look at the day-to-day expenses ("Target" of 60 percent). One way to force this program is to physically move 40 percent into separate accounts (and the next chapter shows exactly how to do it), and once the 40 percent is set aside, just live on the remaining 60 percent.

The heart of the Freedom Money Management System™ is about controlling the flow of money in your life to do what you want it to do without waste.

If a more precise approach is desirable, one can break down the day-to-day expenses into the fixed monthly, variable monthly, and discretionary categories.

In the example, the fixed monthly category has two subcategories: taxes withheld from pay and other items withheld. Many people have more withheld from their paychecks than is necessary with the idea of getting refunds at tax season. You need to withhold only enough to pay your taxes. Getting a refund may seem like a windfall, but in reality you are lending the government YOUR money interest free.

Overall day-to-day expenses have to come down by $1,315 a month to reach the "Target." Simply reallocating this money is the beginning of a sustainable, practical plan.

Your Own Plan

The next step is to decide for yourself how you want to proceed. The Jenkins plan is an idea that has worked for many. By now you should have an idea of what it will take to live within your means and how to repair the mistakes of the past.

The forecasting worksheets in Forms 5.1 and 5.1a may help. Form 5.1 contains suggested expense categories similar to the Jenkins plan; Form 5.1a is blank so you may fill in your own categories. Both forms appear at the end of the chapter and are also downloadable at our Web site: www.ptff.net.

Conclusion

Forecasting can be really tough, particularly if you have a really large amount of debt or weakened income. But, no matter how desperate things may seem for you, remember that someone else who was in far worse shape has worked his or her way out. You need to believe that you can do it and that it is worth doing.

The next chapter, Chapter 6, introduces you to a very simple way to put the plan you have developed into motion and to manage your finances on a day-to-day basis using the power of electronic banking: the Freedom Money Management System™.

Form 5.1   Forecasting Worksheet (with categories)

Date		Target			History			Change to meet target		
Category	%	Annual $	Monthly $	%	Annual $	Monthly $	% (+/-)	Annual $	Monthly $
Permanent savings/retirement										
Escrow set aside for major items										
Day-to-day living expenses >>total										
Sub-totals										
•Fixed										
- -Taxes withheld										
- -Other items withheld										
•Variable										
•Discretionary										
Fun/leisure/recreation										
Get-out-of-debt allocation										
Savings for Goals										
TOTALS	100%			100%						

Note: Shaded areas are sub-totals

Form 5.1 (a)   Forecasting Worksheet (blank)

Date _____

Category	Target			History				Change to meet target		
	%	Annual $	Monthly $	%	Annual $	Monthly $	% (+/-)	Annual $	Monthly $	
TOTALS	100%			100%						

CHAPTER SIX

The Freedom Money Management System™: Powered by On-Line Banking

This chapter is an introduction to the Freedom Money Management System™, a system that is designed specifically to free up your time, eliminate waste in your spending habits, and put you in control of your finances by taking advantage of the power of on-line banking. If your life is filled with conflict and disagreement over finances, you will learn a simple way to end that bickering and stress forever.

This chapter is a complete and freestanding guide to the system. You may start with this chapter no matter what your present financial situation. If, however, you have read and applied the previous five chapters, you are well equipped to move on to the techniques for managing your money on a day-to-day basis presented in this chapter.

Why On-Line Banking Is a Good Idea

If you are old enough, you will remember when no one had a microwave oven. Rumors abounded about the dangers of radiation, and nobody really knew how to cook with the ovens. How different things are now.

Electronic banking today is where microwave cooking was 40 years ago. If you are not using electronic banking and on-line bill paying today, you are missing out on a technological marvel. It is safe, secure, simple, inexpensive, practical, and flexible.

Never again do you need to wonder what your bank balance is, wonder what bills have been paid, wonder whether your paycheck got deposited, lick those dreadful-tasting envelopes, or make trips to the post office for stamps.

You should expect your bank to have *free* on-line bill-paying service. If you pay 15 bills a month by mail at $0.46 per stamp, that adds up to a savings of over $80 a year in postage alone.

The procedures for using electronic banking vary from bank to bank, but every bank can walk you step by step through the process in less than 15 minutes.

The Purpose of a System

Any system is based on a series of premises, or rules, that if followed assure that the system works. If you understand the underlying rationale of the Freedom Money Management System™, you can easily configure the specific components of the system to meet your individual circumstances and preferences. This flexibility and adaptability make the system both practical and powerful. Systems that do not accommodate your personal needs are abandoned quickly.

Your first choice is either to use a deliberate system or not to use any system and deal with money issues as they arise. Simply put, using a deliberate, systematic process for managing your money increases the probability that you will reach your goals. If your perspective on your life extends beyond today, a system can help you get there. Otherwise you are leaving the outcomes of your future to chance. The choice is yours.

Commitments You Need to Make

Before any system can be useful to you, you must make some value judgments and commitments. The Freedom Money Management System™ is based on these commitments:

- Pay yourself first

- Live within your means

- Get out of debt and stay out of debt

- Plan for the future

- Stick with the program for the long haul

Attributes of Our System

To be successful, a system must:

- Be simple, understandable, flexible, practical, and, after being set up, require very little time to maintain.

- Eliminate stress and conflict over money within the money environment—typically the family unit.

- Control the flow of money so that the funds are used as planned and holes in the money bucket are plugged to eliminate waste. Every dollar of waste eliminated is part of your raise!

- Create barriers that reduce impulse spending, and make it easier to do the right thing than the wrong thing.

- Provide useful and timely information about your finances.

Practical Lessons from History

A Cash Society

Past practices provide some practical guidelines for designing a modern system. In our grandparents' time—not all that long ago—personal checking accounts were relatively uncommon. People used cash. Running out of money was a very real possibility. To prevent this unpleasant situation, many people kept several envelopes to hold cash for important categories: one for the rent or mortgage payment, one for groceries, and other envelopes for whatever further expenditures needed to be controlled. When an envelope was empty, spending in that category stopped until the next payday. Elaborate budgets were largely unnecessary. Experience dictated how much was reasonable to spend and how much had to be reserved for upcoming needs. The temptation to overspend was self-regulating.

The lesson: You should physically sort money into different places to control overspending and to be prepared for upcoming expenses. When all your money is in one "pot," the temptation is ever-present to use it all. The one-pot approach also makes it hard to keep track of balances and difficult to exert control.

This very simple technique of sorting money is powerful and is fundamental to our system. The Freedom Money Management System™ sorts your money into "electronic envelopes."

Early Checking Accounts

When consumer checking accounts became common, the discipline imposed by the possibility of running out of money was still very real. If you wrote a check for the rent with no money in your account, the bank probably returned the check to your landlord marked "insufficient funds." Bouncing a check was embarrassing for you, was costly because of the fees charged, and could be inconvenient because your landlord might not accept your checks in the future.

Easy Credit

Enter the era of easy credit. Overdraft lines with the lure of never running out of money were introduced. Impulse spending had no restraints. The banker now earned substantial fees for your bad habits and was certainly not going to admonish you to rein in your recklessness. Today, your banker will rarely embarrass you by returning a check that you write against insufficient funds. Instead, your account will receive a transfusion of credit and a fee will be assessed. The stigma of bouncing a check may have disappeared, but the consequences of being out of control are still very real.

If you are out of money or out of control and continue to write checks and incur the punishing fees imposed by your banker, you need to change the way you manage your money. Avoiding such fees is one very effective way of giving yourself a raise.

Instant Gratification

Easy credit did more than erode discipline for managing checking accounts; it introduced the concept of Buy Now/Pay Later, which has beome so popular that it is now unusual to Save Now/Buy Later. Why bother to wait?

Older readers will recall when Christmas Club accounts were heavily advertised by the banks. You would sign up for these accounts and make monthly payments to the bank, just as if you were paying on a loan. At the end of the year—just before Christmas—you would get a check from the bank in time for seasonal shopping. Credit cards have made these accounts extinct.

Do you really want to give yourself a raise? Stop using credit and paying interest to someone else. Save before you buy and earn the interest for yourself.

Let's suppose you want a new flat-screen high-definition television set that costs $1,500. You put it on your credit card, which charges you 14 percent interest, and promise yourself that you will pay it off in full in two years. That seems reasonable enough. Your payments will be $72.02 a month. So the TV really will cost $1,728.46 (you are paying approximately $228 extra in interest).

But that is only half of the equation. If instead you decide to put the $72.02 a month aside in a savings account that earns 4 percent interest and then buy the TV, at the end of two years your savings account will have $1,796.39 (you have earned approximately $296 in interest). The combination of the interest you paid by purchasing on credit and the interest you would earn if you instead saved up for the TV is a significant $524.85.

Instant gratification is very expensive. Live better for a lot less by waiting to buy something until you are able to pay cash for it. The Freedom Money Management System™ is designed to make it easy for you to develop good money management habits.

With history as a perspective, let's continue the process of setting up a working system.

Allocate Your Funds

Getting started requires some decisions before the tools of the system can be selected and configured to your personal profile. First, for planning purposes, it is useful to allocate funds into three spending time frames (once allocated, the funds will then be physically segregated into different spending "buckets"):

- Money to be spent in the FUTURE (pay yourself first)—that is, *permanent savings*

- Money to be spent LATER (within the next five years)—that is, *escrow accumulation*

- Money to be spent NOW (this month or pay period)—that is, *current expenses* (a big clump, which must be broken down further, see below)

Plan the Distribution of Funds

Once funds are allocated to time frames, a more detailed assessment of expenses is necessary. Form 6.1 is a simple worksheet structured to help you sort expenses into sensible monthly payment categories that flow from the three time frames. (A blank of Form 6.1 is shown in Illustration 6.1 and also appears at the end of this chapter, and in addition it may be downloaded from our Web site: www.ptff.net.)

For each item, the following should be decided:

- What item specifically is going to be paid?

- How much is going to be paid?

- How will the payment be made? Payment choices are discussed in detail below, in the section "Choices for Spending Money and Paying Bills."

- Who will be responsible for making the payment?

Let's look at each major spending category in more detail.

FUTURE Spending (Permanent Savings)

At least 10 percent of your gross pay should go into the FUTURE spending bucket. Too many people who want to save money fall into the trap of paying the NOW bills first, planning to save what is left over. The problem is that seldom is anything left over. Such thinking is backwards. Pay yourself first (that is, allocate the money to the FUTURE bucket first—"Permanent Savings" on Form 6.1) and then live on what is left.

LATER Spending (Within the Next Five Years)

Big expenses that cannot be digested within the monthly cash flow need to be saved for a little bit at a time. A $3,600 property tax bill is a budget buster unless you set aside $300 each month so you will have the funds when the bill comes due. The Freedom Money Management System™ includes an escrow account to address such budget busters ("Escrow Accumulation" on Form 6.1; more details later in this chapter). Failure to have the money on hand when it is needed triggers excursions into credit card debt, and that is a very bad idea.

Form 6.1   Monthly Payment Plan

| Items | Amount | How Paid | | | Who Pays? |
		Automatic transfer	Checks or On-line	Cash	
Permanent Savings					
Escrow Accumulation					
Monthly Fixed Expenses					
Monthly Variable Expenses					
Discretionary Expenses					
#1 Personal Funds					
#2 Personal Funds					
TOTALS					

Illustration 6.1   Blank of Form 6.1

NOW Spending

Most of your money will fall into the NOW bucket. Typically, most of these expenses are paid from the household checking account. That is how most families handle bills these days.

As you can see from Form 6.1, these NOW expenses should be broken down into subgroups (monthly fixed; monthly variable; discretionary; personal funds). There are many ways to categorize these expenses, but I have found that the following categories make practical sense because they share common characteristics that suggest the ideal payment method:

- *Monthly fixed* obligations—the amount stays the same every month. These are must-pay bills and cannot be changed easily. Examples: rent or mortgage payments and car loans.

- *Monthly variable* obligations—these are must-pay bills the amount of which varies from month to month. Example: utility bills.

- *Discretionary expenses* that vary in amount and can be postponed. This type of expense offers you the most short-term control and is the most feasible opportunity to cut back spending. Examples: clothing, eating out, entertainment, recreation, vacations, groceries, and, of course, *personal allowances* (or *personal funds*).

I want to stress that **personal allowances are one of the keys to avoiding stress and conflict over money.** Every person in the spending unit, irrespective of their contribution to the incoming funds, MUST have some money that is theirs to do with as they wish. No exceptions! Grandma called it "mad money"; some refer to it as "walking around money" or simply an "allowance." Later, we'll discuss the size of the allowance and how to set up an allowance, but whatever the amount, every person must have personal funds physically set apart from the communal money.

The last entry lines on Form 6.1 are for these personal funds. Each fund should be separated physically. For example, if your unit is a small family of a husband and a wife, you would have three buckets in the "spend it NOW" allocation: His, Hers, and Ours (everything else).

For funds in the Ours bucket there are several ways of making payments. Some choices are better than others, so let's now explore the choices for paying bills.

Choices for Spending Money and Paying Bills

The basic tools and ways for you to spend your money include the following.

Cash

Good old-fashioned cash is highly recommended for discretionary purchases. It is easier to be self-disciplined when spending cash than when using a credit card. When you take the cash out of your pocket and see how much (or how little) is still available, self-discipline magically kicks in.

Automatic Teller Machine (ATM) Cards

An ATM card allows you to withdraw cash directly from your bank account (if the account contains money) via an ATM. ATM networks are everywhere, so access to your cash is rarely a problem. Each ATM is owned by someone, and if that owner is not your bank, the owner may assess a charge for the convenience of using the machine. Some banks also charge you when you use an ATM that is not theirs.

Some merchants that choose not to accept any form of electronic payment (credit cards or debit cards) and insist on cash may have an ATM on site.

Debit Cards

Virtually all banks issue debit cards at the time you open a checking account. While a debit card looks like a credit card and is processed in the same way at the point of purchase, it is actually a check without the paper. When you present a debit card to pay for something, you are spending money you already have in the bank.

Paper Checks

Paper checks are still useful and convenient but are becoming less so. Some small retailers still do not accept credit cards, and many tradesmen (plumbers, for example) prefer cash, will accept a check, but do not take credit cards.

On-Line Banking

On-line banking offers many features and services, one of which is a convenient way of paying bills. You access your account from your computer and select the bill-paying option. You enter the names of the payees (those to whom you wish to make payment) one time. Then you merely select the payee and enter the amount you want to pay and the date you want to pay it. The bank either transfers your funds electronically to the payee if the payee is a major account (such as a utility) or mails a paper check to arrive on the date you specify. During the process you can see exactly how much money you have in your account. The bank maintains a permanent, easily accessible record of all of your payments as well as a list of pending payments.

For accounts paid monthly with variable amounts due, on-line electronic bill paying is the best, fastest, easiest, safest, most convenient, and cheapest way to pay these bills. You have up-to-the-minute access to activity in your accounts 24/7. Also, merchants increasingly offer a discount for paying electronically.

Telephone Transfer

The current banking system allows almost all bills to be paid by telephone transfer (you phone the payee of a bill and arrange for the payee to deduct your payment directly from your checking account). This method is particularly useful when the day before a bill's payment due date you want to pay the bill without incurring a penalty or late fee.

If you are planning to use telephone transfer, review your bank's procedures. Some accounts may not be eligible (either because of regulations, bank policy, or computer program design), and some may incur fees.

Automatic Payments and Automatic Funds Transfer

"Automatic" means that you arrange for your bank to automatically deduct a payment or automatically transfer money on a set schedule. This method is the preferred choice for making fixed monthly payments and transferring funds to other accounts. The process can originate with the merchant or vendor or with the bank. For example, your mortgage holder can automatically charge your account for your monthly mortgage payment. Your bank can set up transfers out of your checking account into a savings account.

Credit Cards

A credit card is a way to *borrow* money. You can use it to pay for goods and services, or you can use it to get a cash advance. The amount you can borrow (your credit limit) is determined by the lender (your bank) at the time the card is issued. Credit cards can be very expensive. You may be charged an annual fee. If you do not pay in full every month, you are charged interest for the amount you have charged (borrowed), usually at a very high rate. If you do not pay on time, there is a fee.

It's easy to overuse credit cards—buying too much and purchasing on impulse—so credit cards are a bad choice for routine purchases. Only use a credit card if there is a compelling reason. Remember that you are not really paying for something when you put it on a credit card, you are going into debt; and by going into debt, you restrict your future financial freedom.

Kinds of Bank Accounts

The Freedom Money Management System™ uses standard bank accounts to simplify and control your money life. The way in which these accounts are linked creates a powerful and easy-to-use system. The accounts utilized in the Freedom Money Management System™ are fully described below.

Banks have "transaction accounts" and "investment accounts." Our system is concerned only with the transaction accounts—that is, accounts that permit you easy access to your money and give you the ability to move the money around simply, promptly, and remotely. Transaction accounts include (1) checking accounts, (2) savings accounts, and (3) money market accounts.

Checking Accounts

Checking accounts are marketed under various options and fee choices by different banks, but they all function identically. Bankers' jargon for these is "demand deposit accounts" (DDAs), which means legally you can get your money back "on demand." You want to have a checking account with the lowest fees or the lowest balance required for zero fees. You want a checking account from a bank that offers *free* on-line banking and electronic bill paying linked to the checking account. If you plan to write lots of checks (bad idea), you may want to know if there is a per-check charge for that service. This seems quite rare today. Most banks no longer return your paper checks. If you need proof of payment (the only possible reason for wanting a cancelled check), the bank will make you a copy from its electronic records.

Funds in a checking account can be accessed by an ATM or debit card or by paper check.

Savings Accounts

In the past, savings accounts were called "passbook savings" because you had to go into the bank and present your passbook to make deposits or withdrawals. Transactions were handwritten into your passbook. The passbook was your literal proof that the bank had your money. Obviously, now all transactions are recorded electronically. Savings accounts typically pay very low interest.

Under current bank regulations, funds in a savings account cannot be accessed by a debit card or by checks, but savings accounts can be accessed with ATM cards. Funds can be transferred by telephone or on line.

Money Market Accounts (MMAs)

Money market accounts are hybrid accounts that evolved years ago when the commercial banking system was being modernized and overhauled. They pay higher interest than traditional savings accounts, access by ATM card is unlimited, and you can write a limited number of checks on MMAs. However, access to your money is restricted in terms of how many transfers can be made or how many checks can be written. These accounts are ideal for holding money that is ultimately earmarked for something else, such as upcoming tuition or property taxes. They are also ideal accounts for accumulating permanent savings until you have enough to put into other investments.

Points to Consider When Selecting a Payment Choice

This section presents this author's preferences and biases, which may differ from those of others.

Automatic Funds Transfer

Clearly, automatic transfers are ideal for

- Pay-yourself-first transfers into a money market account (or other investment account)

- Fixed monthly obligations such as your mortgage or rent and installment loans

- Deposits into other system accounts such as escrow or allowance accounts

On-Line Bill Paying

On-line bill paying works well for paying

- Variable monthly expenses such as utilities

- Discretionary expenses that occur regularly

- Major expenses for which escrow funds have been accumulated

- Nearly all bills for which you previously wrote checks

Checks

I suggest paying by check be limited to

- The rare occasion when setting up an account on line is not worth it

- One-time never-to-recur payments; for example, to a kid selling subscriptions door to door

Debit Cards

Debit cards may be used as follows (but read the cautionary discussion below):

- Instead of cash any time you would use cash

- Instead of a check at a point of purchase such as the grocery store

- Instead of a credit card for catalog or mail-order purchases

Debit cards pose a real dilemma. Some financial security critics simply abhor debit cards and think they are a very bad idea. (See comments in Chapter 9.) Still other experts are completely and unequivocally committed to the debit card and think credit cards are the root of nearly all the world's problems (probably including droughts, tornadoes, and global warming). Neither camp is completely correct. You need to decide the risks and benefits for yourself.

Two significant risks associated with debit cards are *blocking* and *identity theft*. If you use a debit card for a major transaction (let's say a one-week car rental while on vacation), the merchant will contact the card issuer and "block" an amount estimated to be what you will owe when you settle up. This blocked amount may make unavailable enough funds that you may inadvertently overdraw your account.

If you lose your debit card and it is used by an identity thief, it may be some time before you are aware of it. Meanwhile, the money in your account and any linked accounts (including credit lines) may be drained before you have any notice. While recent changes to the law and banks' policies may protect you from fraudulent use, it may take a long time to resolve the situation and get your money back.

A final caution: this author has experienced less than satisfactory results in getting credited funds back into his checking account for returned goods when they were purchased with a debit card.

Cash

I recommend you use cash for

- All day-to day items such as lunch, haircuts, parking, etc.

- Groceries and household supplies

- Recreation and entertainment

Cash is really effective in controlling impulse spending, and therefore this author has a very strong bias for using cash whenever possible. This is particularly true if your cash allocation is finite—that is, you have a certain amount of cash for a certain amount of time or for a certain event and you have no way to recharge your stash. When what you have is gone, there is no more.

Two examples make the point. You have $40 cash and it has to last the rest of the week. What is the likelihood that you will splurge for the prime rib for lunch at $14.95, plus drinks, dessert, tax, and a tip, for a total tab of $23.15? If it is Monday, you probably will settle for less; if it is Friday, you may live a little large to end the week.

Some recreational gamblers I know set aside a specific bundle of cash when they head for the casino. When it is gone, the excursion is over. They have enough discipline not to break the rules they have set for themselves.

Credit Cards

Credit cards are not a way to pay bills. They are a way to borrow money to convert one bill into a different bill while simultaneously increasing the price you are paying for anything. (Unless, of course, you pay the account in full on time every month.)

There are many proponents of credit cards and a seemingly equal number of advisors who oppose them. If you are out of control with spending that is driven by easy credit, it makes sense to take away the piece of plastic that is letting you get away with it. People on a diet do well to keep Ben and Jerry's exotic high-calorie ice cream out of the house. Research has shown repeatedly that people spend more when they can simply swipe a card instead of counting out the cash. Credit cards magically remove the natural inhibitions favoring frugality.

However, credit cards can be a good idea to use for some transactions:

- Mail or catalog purchases—purchasing with a credit card simplifies returns if you are dissatisfied

- Travel expenses: car rentals, airline tickets, and hotels—a credit card company often extends insurance coverage when the rental is charged to its card

- Business expenses

- Major purchases—warranties are often extended when a purchase is charged

One more time: Do not use credit cards to buy things you cannot afford! You cannot afford something if you do not have the funds now to pay cash for it.

The Freedom Money Management System™

The Freedom Money Management System™ is designed to take advantage of on-line banking and to segregate funds into different "electronic envelopes" using standard kinds of bank accounts.

Illustration 6.2 is a flow chart showing how to set up the most basic system using three separate accounts: a primary checking account, a money market account, and a savings account.

The Basic Three-Account System

Primary Checking

Start with a *checking account* that offers free on-line electronic banking. This checking account is the primary account into which all income is deposited (preferably by direct deposit) and from which the bulk of your bills and expenses are paid. Automatic transfers are made out of this account into the other accounts.

A Pay-Yourself-First Retirement Account

Open a *money market account* (MMA) and use it to *pay yourself first* by automatically transferring predetermined amounts from the primary checking account into it every month.

Personal Savings Accounts

Open a basic *personal savings account* with ATM card access to this account. Estimate how much you will need for expenses you pay with cash. This amount is your "allowance." Have this amount transferred automatically from your checking account into this savings account—probably to coincide with your paydays. (Note: Later in this chapter I discuss how much should go into this account and the option to make it a secondary checking account rather than a savings account.)

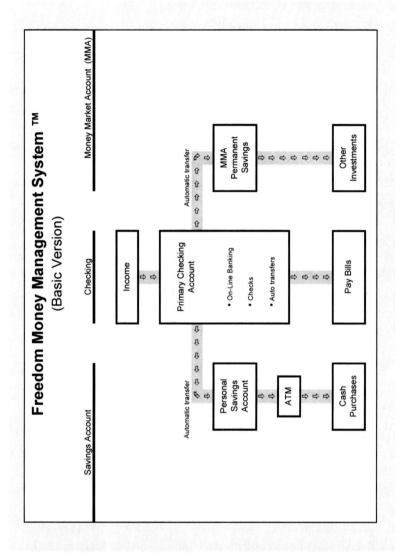

Illustration 6.2   Flow Chart of Basic Freedom Money Management System™

The Recommended Four-Account System:
When You Need an Escrow Account

When life becomes more complicated than simply paying for things from paycheck to paycheck, you need a way to accumulate funds for upcoming major expenses. The best way to accomplish this is through an escrow account that physically separates funds that you *intend to spend* in the future from your day-to-day life.

To accomplish this in our system is simple. Just add another money market account for escrow funds to the basic three-account system.

Although you could achieve this goal by drawing from your investment accounts, that is a bad habit. Investment accounts are not intended for short-term expenses. Keep investment funds separated from funds you plan to spend.

Anticipating upcoming expenses and saving for them in advance also eliminates the temptation (or necessity) of using debt to pay the bills. As a comic once said, "The only way to eat an elephant is one bite at a time." If you take the known future expenses and deal with them "one bite at a time," you will not need to borrow to pay them.

An expanded discussion of the escrow account, along with planning forms with examples, appears later in this chapter.

The Family System—Five or More Accounts

Illustration 6.3 shows the Freedom Money Management System™ set up for a family. To implement the *family* system—to accommodate more than one spender—all you need do is set up a savings account with ATM access for each person who gets an allowance from the family cash. This individual savings account puts each person in charge of his/her own spending without direct access to the primary checking account. An agreed-upon amount is automatically transferred into an individual's savings account from the primary checking account.

Financial conflict affects many families, causes stress, and is one of the leading causes of divorce. When more than one person in the family is involved with money, it is imperative that the origins of family conflict about money be addressed.

No two people have the same spending habits, spending priorities, or spending styles. Ending financial conflict begins by examining where

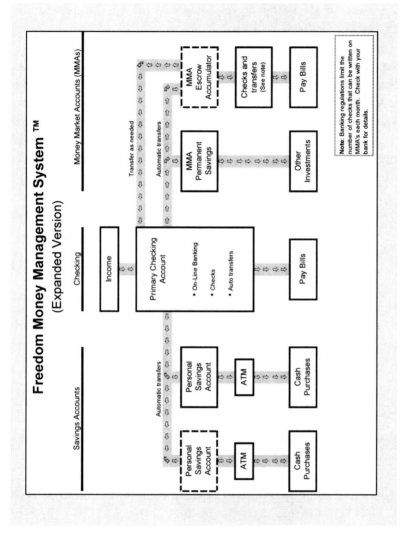

Illustration 6.3   The Family Freedom Money Management System™

money has gone in the past and estimating where it will go in the future. It continues with goal setting among family members.

It is important to recognize that each family member needs some money to spend any way and any time that person wants without answering to anyone else (unless they want to)—a personal "allowance" or walking around money. My grandmother called it her "mad money." I think she meant that when she was mad at grandpa, she could go and treat herself to get over it. It is reassuring to have money in your pocket. It is even more so if you never have any reason to feel guilty about how and where you spend it.

These personal savings accounts are used for cash purchases. Obviously, the amounts will differ with each individual and family. Open negotiation and candid discussion will lead to an agreed amount for each person. This approach eliminates conflict, reduces stress, and encourages wise spending habits. From time to time the amounts need to be reviewed for fairness and adequacy. This communication alone is vital to reducing conflict and stress.

By using the power of the banking system with its cluster of accounts, you can almost put money management on autopilot. Once you have set up your system, an hour a month is more than enough time to stay in complete control of your finances.

How Much Should You Escrow?

How much should you set aside in an escrow account? Once you know the amount you will need, or can estimate it, and you determine how many months remain before you have to pay out the money, you just need to divide the amount into monthly chunks to determine how much to escrow each month. Form 6.2 will help you plan escrowing activities (a blank of the form appears at the end of this chapter as well as on our Web site, www.ptff.net).

Take a look at the Illustrations 6.4A and 6.4B (copies of Form 6.2 with sample data) to see how escrowing works with three simple examples.

Example 1: Property taxes of $6,000 will be due October 1, 2010, and you start setting aside money in April (Illustration 6.4A). This means you will need to set aside $1,000 a month for the next six months. Since the same property taxes can be expected next year and you will have 12 months to set aside money, you will only need to set aside $500 a month after this year's taxes are paid (shown in Illustrations 6.4A and 6.4B).

This example flows over into the following year (Illustration 6.4 B). Note that the "Balance Forward" column shows you will already have $1,000 going into the next year for property tax escrow. Notice the running total (balance) line that shows how much you will have set aside if you follow the program.

Example 2: You estimate that a really nice vacation in 2014 will cost $9,000. Of course, you could put everything on a credit card and be paying for the trip for two or three years after you have made the memories. With interest, the vacation could end up costing you more like $12,000. Paying for the vacation on credit is a bad idea unless you do not need an extra $3,000, the raise you could "give" yourself by escrowing the money instead of paying on credit.

By starting in August 2013 and setting aside $750 a month, you will be able to pay cash for the vacation.

Example 3: If your goal for 2016 is to buy an ATV for $9,000, you will need to start saving $250 a month in July of 2013.

Finally, total up the amount you need to set aside each month for all three examples ("Cumulative Total" line at the foot of Form 6.2). The further ahead you plan, the smaller the monthly escrow amount. If you cannot set aside the amount you need, you have to reassess your goals or readjust your day-to-day expenses OR go into debt. If you choose going into debt, you will be foregoing part of that raise you were going to give yourself, once again giving up some of your financial freedom.

The escrow planning experience will help you get away from a financial life dominated by crisis and significantly reduces stress. The forms and the process are simple, and the payoff in peace of mind is enormous.

Variations on the Savings (Allowance) Account(s)

Let's get back to basics. Three key purposes drive the personal savings (personal allowance) account. The first is to physically isolate these funds from the overall pool of funds. The second is to drive home the concept that there is only so much money available and when it is gone, it is gone. It is this enforced discipline that people without credit cards really understand. The third purpose is to provide each person with some truly personal money that is his or hers to spend in any way he or she wants. The end result is a reduction of stress and conflict.

Form 6.2   Escrow Account Worksheet For Year: ___2013___

Items		Bal. Fwd	Jan	Feb	Mar	Apr	May	Jun	Jul	Aug	Sep	Oct	Nov	Dec
Property Taxes	Add to					1000	1000	1000	1000	1000	1000		500	500
	Deduct											(6000)		
	Balance					1000	2000	3000	4000	5000	6000	0	500	1000
Vacation 2014	Add to									750	750	750	750	750
	Deduct													
	Balance									750	1500	2250	3000	3750
Goal: Buy ATV	Add to								250	250	250	250	250	250
June 2016	Deduct													
$9,000	Balance								250	500	750	1000	1250	1500
	Add to													
	Deduct													
	Balance													
	Add to													
	Deduct													
	Balance													
	Add to													
	Deduct													
	Balance													
	Add to													
	Deduct													
	Balance													
	Add to													
	Deduct													
	Balance													
	Add to													
	Deduct													
	Balance													
Cumulative Total	Add to					1000	1000	1000	1250	2000	2000	1000	1500	1500
	Deduct											(6000)		
	Balance					1000	2000	3000	4250	6250	8250	3250	4750	6250

Illustration 6.4A   Form 6.2 with Sample Data

Form 6.2 Escrow Account Worksheet For Year: 2014

Item		Bal. Fwd	Jan	Feb	Mar	Apr	May	Jun	Jul	Aug	Sep	Oct	Nov	Dec
Property Taxes	Add to		500	500	500	500	500	500	500	500	500	500	500	500
	Deduct											(6000)		
	Balance	1000	1500	2000	2500	3000	3500	4000	4500	5000	5500	0	500	1000
Vacation 2014	Add to		750	750	750	750	750	750	750					
	Deduct								(9000)					
	Balance	3750	4500	5250	6000	6750	7500	8250	0					
Goal: Buy ATV June 2016 $9,000	Add to		250	250	250	250	250	250	250	250	250	250	250	250
	Deduct													
	Balance	1500	1750	2000	2250	2500	2750	3000	3250	3500	3750	4000	4250	4500
Cumulative Total	Add to		1500	1500	1500	1500	1500	1500	1500	750	750	750	750	750
	Deduct								(9000)			(6000)		
	Balance	6250	7750	9250	10750	12250	13750	15250	7750	8500	9250	4000	4750	5500

Illustration 6.4B Form 6.2 with Sample Data

If the allowance account is set up as a savings account, the most convenient way to get money is to use an ATM. Of course, you could also go into the bank and make a withdrawal at the counter.

Some proponents of these separate "it's your money" accounts suggest expanding them to include all of the expenses and purchases for which a person is responsible. Let's use groceries as a hypothetical. One person in the family agrees to be responsible for grocery shopping. The periodic grocery allocation (budget amount) is deposited to that person's allowance account in addition to walking around money. The person's obligation is to buy groceries within the budget. If he or she is frugal and shops wisely, some money may be saved. So long as the family is not protesting a diet of two-day-old bread and Hamburger Helper for all meals, the savings are that person's for discretionary use.

For this idea to work, there has to be really sound family trust and open communication. The personal allowance amounts will need to be revisited and revised regularly to fine tune the system for fairness.

If you decide to do this, I suggest that the allowance account be a secondary checking account instead of a savings account, since under current law only a checking account can have both ATM and debit card access.

Where Does Income Get Deposited?

Usually in the Freedom Money Management System™, all income is directly deposited into the primary checking account. From this account, automatic distributions are made to other accounts, including money market accounts for escrow and permanent savings.

As an alternative, you may directly deposit income into an investment account and then have a set amount transferred from there into the primary checking account. Many stock brokerage firms have investment accounts with check-writing options. In order for this approach to make sense, you must have a situation in which only a small portion of your income is needed for living expenses. If you are living on 70 percent or less of your income, consider having all income go directly to your investment account. If you use this approach, you will not need the two money market accounts for escrowed funds and investments.

In this scenario, once or twice a month you transfer out of the investment account into the primary checking account for paying bills. Although you could simply use the investment account (with its checking and on-line privileges) as the primary checking account, I do not like the idea of having long-term money available for day-to-day spending.

Emergency Fund

The ideal place to accumulate an emergency fund is in your escrow money market account (MMA#2). Leading financial experts recommend that you have an amount set aside for emergencies equal to at least six months' expenses. A set-aside of twelve months' expenses is even better. Money, or rather the lack of it, is a major cause of stress and depression.

Instead of drugs, the world's best antidepressant is money in the bank. When you have a reserve of cash that is not already earmarked for anything specific, the peace of mind and financial freedom that result are unlike anything else.

Overdraft Protection

Bounce a check and you are charged a punishing fee. To help you avoid this and incur only a smaller fee, banks offer overdraft (OD) protection by linking your checking account to other sources of funds. These links can be to any other accounts in the bank including your credit card.

But why would anyone need OD protection? If you need such protection, either you do not know how much money is in your account, which is inexcusable, or you write a check anyway, which is also inexcusable. You are either out of control or out of money.

Think about this. When was the last time you ran out of gas in your car? Probably never or a long time ago. Why is this? The car has a gas gauge that tells you how much fuel you have left, and you clearly know the consequences of running out. So you do not run on an empty tank!

A really powerful benefit of on-line banking is that you can see instantly how much money you have in every account. Think of your on-line bank service as your money fuel gauge. If the tank is running dry, transfer money from a money market account into your checking account. If you have an escrow MMA and keep an emergency reserve fund, you should never need OD protection.

If you absolutely insist that you need OD protection, limit that link to one other account and NOT to your credit card.

Will the System Work?

The success of this program depends on a serious commitment to taking charge of your financial life, getting out of debt, staying out of debt, and living within your means. It also assumes a solid family structure and openness to discussing and resolving differences. No marriage will survive hidden indulgences or suspicions between spouses.

This program is flexible in its application provided there is candor and accord from the very beginning. If an "it's mine" possessiveness dominates the spending of money, why bother to be married? Sharing does not have to be in equal in dollars, but it must be open.

The days of grandpa handing out an allowance to a compliant spouse are in the past. If that is your circumstance, this book cannot help you. You have built in stress, friction, and discord by choice. Deal with that first. Money is one cause, if not the leading cause, of divorce. In this author's opinion, it's not the money. Money is simply the element that reveals a basic lack of communication skills. Our system is designed to make communication very simple and practical.

The next chapter deals with getting out of debt. It is important for everyone involved to see how both the money management system and the get-out-of-debt program are leading to success. A lifetime of happiness and stress-free living is the prize.

≫ *A Case for Electronic Bill Paying* ≪

A friend of mine manages her elderly family's finances and pays their bills. One month when the gasoline credit card bill came in, she was shocked to see that the total charges for the past two months exceeded $1,000. My friend knew that one or two gasoline fill-ups cover all of the limited driving her dad does each month. Even with soaring prices at the pump this amount was excessive.

It appeared that there was some fraudulent use of her father's credit card, so she needed to gather all of the information to challenge the charges. It took less than 10 minutes to retrieve and print out the past six months' detailed electronic statements of the gasoline credit card activity. These statements were evidence of a clear pattern that her dad always purchased gas at the same station. The records of the current bill showed several fill-ups on the same day at different locations and at places he never went.

Having this kind of readily accessible history is very useful when you need to put together a case for misuse and avoid becoming liable for fraudulent charges.

Form 6.1   Monthly Payment Plan

Items	Amount	How Paid			Who Pays?
		Automatic transfer	Checks or On-line	Cash	
Permanent Savings					
Escrow Accumulation					
Monthly Fixed Expenses					
Monthly Variable Expenses					
Discretionary Expenses					
#1 Personal Funds					
#2 Personal Funds					
TOTALS					

Form 6.2   Escrow Account Worksheet For Year: _____

Item		Bal. Fwd	Jan	Feb	Mar	Apr	May	Jun	Jul	Aug	Sep	Oct	Nov	Dec
Item	Add to													
	Deduct													
	Balance													
Item	Add to													
	Deduct													
	Balance													
Item	Add to													
	Deduct													
	Balance													
Item	Add to													
	Deduct													
	Balance													
Item	Add to													
	Deduct													
	Balance													
Item	Add to													
	Deduct													
	Balance													
Item	Add to													
	Deduct													
	Balance													
Item	Add to													
	Deduct													
	Balance													
Item	Add to													
	Deduct													
	Balance													
Cumulative Total	Add to													
	Deduct													
	Balance													

CHAPTER SEVEN

Debt Management

Why Debt Is Bad for You

A debt-free life is the foundation of giving yourself a raise. Debt is a prison you build around yourself. You are held hostage to decisions you made in the past. That is, when you buy something and do not pay for it at the time of purchase and the time ultimately comes that you must pay for it, you have previously forfeited the freedom of choice to spend your current dollars on something else. Furthermore, the interest you are paying on your indebtedness is someone else's income. Wouldn't you rather have that money for yourself?

Money issues are bad for your health. They cause stress and depression. They put a strain on personal relationships and are the leading cause of divorce. Money in the bank is one of the most powerful antidepressants in the world. The peace of mind that comes when you know you can pay your bills and have the freedom to make day-to-day choices with current income has unimaginable benefits.

You give up current choices when you buy on credit. But equally serious, everything you buy on credit costs more because you are overlaying the purchase price with interest on the money you are borrowing by purchasing on credit.

In previous chapters, you learned how to set up a spending plan and control system. Part of that plan is to allocate a portion of your income to paying your debt, but until you complete this chapter, the amount you should be allocating cannot be determined with certainty. Let's see how you can balance income, pay current expenses, and pay off yesterday's bills.

If you have no debt, congratulations! You can skip this chapter (or you can share the information in this chapter with someone else and help him/her know the joys of a debt-free life style).

Debt Addiction

If you are still convinced that you simply cannot live debt free, you need to address that fallacy. Rationalizing being in debt is self-destructive behavior that will lead to ever-worsening results.

In 1908, Thorstein Veblen published *The Theory of the Leisure Class*, the classic work in which the term "conspicuous consumption" first appeared. Among the premises he set forth was the idea that certain people simply need some kind of certificate of status. For example, to bolster their own social images, rich women traveled to Europe to marry poor but titled European men (dukes, barons, princes, and the like).

Today, some people mistakenly equate their personal significance or worth with the material trappings around them. An automobile can get you there or show that you have gotten there. How important is the brand name to you?

Myth   I can work my way out of my financial dilemmas without changing how I do things.

Fact   The activities and behavior patterns that got you into an unsatisfactory financial situation will definitely not get you out of the mess. You will have to do something different in the future—probably a lot different if you are deeply in debt. If you always do what you have always done, you will always get what you have always gotten!

Solution   Admit that you will have to change and do not procrastinate about getting started.

Stand on a busy street corner and see how much you can learn about the character of the people passing by from the shoes they are wearing, their watches, suits, coats, jewelry, or anything else material. Not much. More importantly, most of those same people are completely indifferent to the kind of car you drive, the brand name of your washing machine, or anything else about the stuff in your life.

Why are *you* in debt? Are you an addict of conspicuous consumption or is there some other excuse? There are as many excuses as there are people in debt. The simple answer is that you have spent money that you did not have.

Blame the Credit Card

Some authors blame easy credit and the proliferation of credit cards for our indebtedness problems. They advocate destroying all of your credit cards to remove the temptation to buy on credit.

Think of someone on a diet. A good strategy for the dieter is to avoid buying tempting high-calorie foods. If no ice cream is in the freezer, it is less likely that you will be tempted to indulge yourself. This method certainly will work with credit cards (no credit cards equals less temptation), but in my opinion, destroying credit cards simply avoids dealing with the underlying problem of personal self-control and accountability that got you into debt in the first place.

Destroying your credit cards to get out of debt is like blaming the pots and pans and dishes in your kitchen for causing you to get fat. Have you heard of a "break-all-the-dishes" diet plan? Of course not, because it is obviously silly.

By all means make it difficult to use your credit cards, but chopping them up is not the answer. The problem is simply greater than that.

Steps for Getting out of Debt

The three steps for getting out of debt are straightforward:

Step 1:   Live within your means, starting right now. If the total money coming in is less than the money going out, something has to change—NOW!

Step 2: Do not charge anything. To get out of debt, you first have to stop getting into debt. If you are in the debt "hole," stop digging!

Step 3: Set up a debt retirement and monitoring system to keep track of, control, and report on the success of your "get-out-of-debt" program.

This chapter shows you how to set up and maintain an easy control system (step three), and it is very important to have a system. A system keeps you informed of exactly where you are, it shows your progress to keep you from getting discouraged, and it keeps you on track. You need to stay motivated, and a scorekeeping system helps do that.

I recommend three worksheets to help you "keep score":

1. Creditor Worksheet (Form 7.1)

2. Monthly Minimum Payment Summary (Form 7.2)

3. Debt Summary (Form 7.3)

Myth   I am so far in the hole that there is no way I am ever going to get out.

Fact   You can succeed in getting out of debt and living within your means if you are serious about doing it. It will not necessarily be easy or quick, but it is possible.

Solution   First, complete an analysis of everything you spent for the past year (I talked about this in Chapter 3). Next, set up a comprehensive goal list for both your immediate and long-term plan (think as if you had a magic wand). Finally, start an action plan of one little step toward success at a time.

Visit my Web site (www.ptff.net) for examples of how debt reduction works. There you can download Excel files of all the above forms to simplify tracking your progress.

Creditor Worksheet (Form 7.1)

You should fill in one Creditor Worksheet *for each of your creditors* and update the worksheet every month. Keeping the Creditor Worksheets makes you pay attention to just how big your debt is, see what the trend is, and notice when you begin to pay off debt. I promise that seeing you are paying off debt will motivate you to continue. Ignoring your debt is the very worst thing you can do.

A blank of Form 7.1 appears at the end of this chapter and also, as with all forms, can be downloaded from our Web site (www.ptff.net). Or feel free to create your own version of the worksheet.

Illustration 7.1 shows a blank Creditor Worksheet (Form 7.1). As you can see, the worksheet is similar to a checkbook register. Here's how to use the form. When a credit card statement (or loan statement) comes in, transcribe information from the statement to the worksheet as follows:

1. Enter the "date" and the "previous balance" in columns 1 and 2.

2. Enter the "new charges" (if you are following the steps outlined above and you have stopped charging, the "new charges" will be *zero*).

3. Enter the "finance charges"—that is, any interest and fees you are being charged (once you erase your debt, this money will be yours again—you will have given yourself a raise!).

4. Enter the "current balance" (it should be a total of "previous balance," "new charges," and "finance charges").

5. Enter the "minimum payment."

6. When you pay the bill, enter the "amount paid" and then subtract that amount from the new "total due" to get the "new balance."

Note that the "new balance" becomes the "previous balance" when you receive the next statement.

This exercise serves two purposes. First, the worksheet keeps you focused on those nasty interest charges—money that is going to somebody else

Form 7.1   Creditor Worksheet

Creditor: _____   Interest Rate: _____   Credit Line: _____

Date	Previous Balance	New Charges	Finance Charges	Current Balance	Minimum Payment	Amount Paid

Illustration 7.1   Blank Form 7.1

instead of going to you (your future "raise" if you erase your debt). And second, keeping up with the worksheet creates the discipline of reviewing statements to be sure all transactions are correct and accurate. Did you get appropriate credit for returns, is someone else charging on your account, was your payment received on time to avoid late charges and fees?

Monthly Minimum Payment Summary (Form 7.2)

Now sort all the Creditor Worksheets (Form 7.1) by largest "new balance" to smallest.

On the Monthly Minimum Payment Summary form (Form 7.2) list all of your creditors in order (largest to smallest) and for each creditor list the "interest rate," "minimum payment due," and "current balance."

Total the "minimum payment due" column. *You must pay at least this amount.* Look back at your spending plan. Do you have enough to at least pay the minimums? (If not, you must revise your spending—see below.) Also record how much you paid on each bill in the final column. As your bills come in each month, make a new summary form. Illustration 7.2 shows a blank of Form 7.2, and the form also appears at the end of this chapter.

Review and Revise

Once you fill out Form 7.2, you have a clear idea of the absolute minimum total amount you must pay every month. Form 6.1 (Monthly Payment Plan) has a category for "Monthly Variable Expenses." If you haven't already entered credit card payments on that form, do it now. The monthly minimum is the lowest amount you must pay, but to get out of debt in a reasonable time period, you will have to allocate more money to repaying existing debt.

Obviously if you have more money going out than is coming in, you will have to review all of your outgoing funds to see where you can cut back. Nobody can do this for you, and it may take several attempts before you come up with your workable plan. But you must do it.

On One Account Pay More Than the Minimum

Once you've adjusted your spending to have some "excess money," the next step is to use that money to pay down more than the minimum on *one* credit account. Which account should you pay off first? Experts disagree. Some

Form 7.2   Monthly Minimum Payment Summary

Month of: _____				
Creditor	Interest Rate	Minimum Payment Due	Current Balance	Amount Paid
1				
2				
3				
4				
5				
6				
7				
8				
9				
10				
11				
12				
13				
14				
15				
16				
17				
18				
19				
20				
Totals				

Illustration 7.2   Blank Form 7.2

say pay off the one with the highest interest rate first because it is costing you the most. Others advocate first paying off the one with the smallest balance because the psychological lift you get from seeing one PAID is highly motivating. The latter is my bias. Pay off the ones with the lowest balances first, just to see progress. When an account is paid off, apply the minimum you would have paid on that account to the next account on your list.

At bill-paying time, pay the "minimum payment due" on all accounts except the one you are trying to pay off first. Pay more on that account to get rid of it—forever.

> **Myth** When real estate prices improve and the value of my house goes up, I can refinance or take out a home equity loan and my problems will be behind me.
>
> **Fact** Consolidating debt without first examining how you got into it merely shifts dealing with the underlying problems into the future.
>
> **Solution** Assume that your house will never bail you out. Stop going deeper into debt and begin a comprehensive "get-out-of-debt" program.

How much more than the minimum should you pay? The answer depends on how serious you are about getting out of debt. If you are really serious, you will be very aggressive in cutting expenses and using that money to pay off the debt. The daily lattes may disappear. You may eat out less often. Endless opportunities to cut back will come to mind.

Every little bit helps, but do not be so severe that you are in constant misery. The process of getting out of debt should be very rewarding and something about which you should be very proud.

About Fixed Payment Loans

The preceding credit discussion has been about "lines of credit" in which the amount varies from month to month. A line of credit has a credit limit attached to it. Within that limit, you may borrow and repay and the line renews itself. For example, if you have a $7,500 line of credit with your credit card and charge $4,000, you have $3,500 remaining available credit. Pay off $2,000 of the charges and you have renewed that amount and now have $5,500 available credit. Home equity "lines" work the same way.

A loan (as contrasted with a "line") does not renew the original amount as it is paid off. A car loan is an example. If you buy a car for $25,000 with a $5,000 down payment, an interest rate of 6.5 percent, and a six-year term, your payments will be approximately $336 a month. It is more difficult to

Form 7.3   Debt Summary

Current Balance (from Form 7.1)

Creditor	Jan	Feb	Mar	Apr	May	Jun	Jul	Aug	Sep	Oct	Nov	Dec
Total												

Illustration 7.3   Blank of Form 7.3

calculate how to pay off a car early. One technique is to set money aside in savings with the express purpose of paying off the car early.

Home mortgage statements always have an option to pay additional principal at any time. If you are planning to pay off your mortgage early, simply add an amount to each payment. Each monthly statement will give you a summary of your progress.

Summarize and Track Your Progress (Form 7.3)

As a final step in tracking your "get-out-of-debt" program, every month for all creditors transfer the outstanding "new balance" amounts from the Creditor Worksheets (Form 7.1) to the Debt Summary (Form 7.3). The version of this form I supply starts with January and runs through December, but you should redo the form to begin in the month you are starting this exercise.

Put the creditors in descending order by amount of balance, with the creditor with the largest balance first. This year-long form is a recap of your debt reduction progress (Illustration 7.3 is a blank of Form 7.3, which also appears at the end of this chapter). When you see "zero" as the balance next to a creditor's name, celebrate! Give yourself an affordable treat! It took you a long time to get into debt. It may take a long time to get out, but once you are out of debt, you will experience a real sense of freedom.

Monthly Update

Each month update the three worksheets in the system and enter the new balances. Updating is important to keep your motivation high and to see your progress. Equally important, remember to review incoming bills for accuracy. You can detect identity theft early on by noticing unauthorized charges on your credit.

Next

Now that you have a system for managing your money and getting out of debt, it is time to explore more things that have an impact on your financial life. Chapter 8 offers spending strategies to help you get more satisfaction for every dollar you spend, and Chapter 9 delves into the intricacies of credit cards and debit cards.

Form 7.1   Creditor Worksheet

Creditor:

Interest Rate:

Credit Line:

Date	Previous Balance	New Charges	Finance Charges	Current Balance	Minimum Payment	Amount Paid

Form 7.2   Minimum Payment Summary

Creditor	Interest Rate	Minimum Payment Due	Current Balance	Amount Paid
Month of: _____				
1				
2				
3				
4				
5				
6				
7				
8				
9				
10				
11				
12				
13				
14				
15				
16				
17				
18				
19				
20				
Totals				

Form 7.3   Debt Summary

Current Balance (from Form 7.1)

Creditor	Jan	Feb	Mar	Apr	May	Jun	Jul	Aug	Sep	Oct	Nov	Dec
Total												

CHAPTER EIGHT

Spending Strategies

Why You Buy

Uncontrolled spending and impulse spending are some of the main reasons for increased debt and its inevitable financial stress. If you cannot control your spending, you will never achieve your financial goals.

So, before we delve into tips and techniques that only deal with the symptoms of excessive spending, let's explore the dynamics and psychology of spending.

Why do you buy (and we concede the fact that spending money is fun for most people)? The simple answer is to satisfy a need. But what exactly is that need, and how can understanding what we refer to as needs help us formulate our own spending strategies?

Every purchase can be broken into two components.

- *The first component is function.* What exactly does the thing or service being purchased do?

- *The second component is psychological.* What is the emotional meaning of the purchase? It is this second component that concerns us the most. Marketers spend billions of dollars every year with the sole objective of making you believe that their products or services are the best and, furthermore, that you deserve them. Once this perception becomes your reality, your rational decision making is compromised. Your temptation is to ignore the cost and feed your ego.

Nothing is better than feeling good about what you bought. And nothing is worse than feeling dissatisfied with your purchase soon after you buy it. (Marketing professionals refer to this phenomenon as "cognitive dissonance," that is, literally awareness that on hindsight you may have made the wrong choice.)

The Psychological Component: Building Impulse Immunity

The purpose of learning about the psychological component of buying is to develop an immunity to making irrational purchases on the basis of the emotional appeal of the item. I intend no judgment about what you should or should not buy. Your decisions about how to spend your money are up to you. What I do intend is that you become aware of the forces acting on you when you are shopping. The consistent theme throughout this book is that your value as a person is not defined by the stuff you own. Self-image is not bought with stuff.

Myth   People look up to you when you have the right stuff.

Fact   Your personal self-worth is not measured by the possessions you have or don't have. Mr. T, the *A-Team* actor notorious for wearing an enormous collar of gold, said, when interviewed about a concern for being robbed, "I am never going to cry over something that cannot cry for me."

Solution   Ask yourself, "Do I own my stuff or does it own me?"

Myth Being able to go out and spend whatever I want whenever I want makes me feel good.

Fact Instant gratification is a form of immaturity. You definitely need to grow up when it comes to your money. If buying something (anything) has become a pattern to get a "feel good" lift, you need to deal with this inappropriate retail therapy. Chronic dependency on instant gratification becomes long-term misery. This outcome is especially likely if retail therapy is financed with credit and growing indebtedness.

Solution As with any addiction, you may need help to break the bad habits of an addiction to retail therapy. Once you recognize that you are spending money just for the sake of the immediate satisfaction the spending gives you, you can develop strategies to limit your impulse spending and find other sources of satisfaction.

Think for a moment about a purchase that on reflection you wish you had not made. Why did you buy the item and, if the purchase was on credit and you are still paying for it, how does that make you feel now?

The beginning of shopping wisdom is to understand yourself and what drives you to buy. You alone can assess the value you derive from any purchase. But what you might want to do is a little honest self-assessment to test your own values. "Why am I buying this?" is a good opening question. Let's look at a few product examples for practice.

Wristwatches

The wristwatch is a good item to use to explore function versus ego. What does a watch do? It tells time. Setting aside special-purpose watches (such as scuba divers' watches or timers), the only *use* for a watch is telling time. How much did you pay for your watch? If you paid anything over $10, you paid for something other than function. For $10 at any Wal-Mart, Target, or drug store, you can purchase a watch that is thousands of times more accurate than any watch you could have purchased at any price 100 years ago. Back then, if accuracy was important to you, you had to pay a lot more. Now accuracy is a given. Now, more money does not get you a more accurate watch.

But, you may well say, I wouldn't wear a $10 watch. Why not? Every reason you can assert for spending more than $10 is simply rationalization. Nothing wrong, mind you, with liking style, the jewelry look, the approval of your friends, or the mere pleasure of owning something you perceive as "fine." But understand, you are paying for psychological value, not function. Again, I am not suggesting you avoid spending money on a fine watch. I am trying to help you understand that in every purchase you have choices—some rational, some emotional.

Cell Phones

Cell phones are another popular purchase the cost of which can range from a free phone when you contract for a certain period of service to many hundreds of dollars for a phone. The pride of owning the most sophisticated, up-to-date technology may tempt you into spending much more for a unit than your functional needs warrant. Again, you choose how best to spend your money, but cutting-edge technology is rarely the best buy. Being the "first kid on the block" to own something new and trendy is purely emotional.

Automobiles

For most people, automobiles are the largest expense in their lives other than their homes. No industry focuses more intensely on the psychological elements of the purchase decision than the auto industry. An auto manufacturer's intent is to make its brand part of your cultural values. Merchandising is a two-pronged effort. You are made to feel that you belong to a select group if you buy the brand, or you are made to feel inadequate (or some other less desirable trait) among your friends if you have the wrong brand.

That merchandising gets you to the automobile dealership where you believe there is a "fit," and then carefully trained salespeople build on those cultural values. In addition, car salespeople are masters at selling you a car with a higher price tag than you think you can afford by suggesting you finance the purchase and manipulating the monthly loan payment to an illusorily low amount (that is, they convince you to focus on the size of the monthly payment rather than on the fact that you are increasing the purchase cost with interest).

However, borrowing money for a car is a habit you should try to break. Keeping an affordable car for a long period allows you the opportunity to accumulate cash for the next car purchase so that you can avoid financing your next car. Instead of paying interest, you will be paying yourself.

Buying for emotional satisfaction is only one facet of the car-buying process. Understanding your emotions will help you shop more wisely when you look at the features you want to buy. (Just try to keep emotions separate during the analysis process.)

Other Facets of Car Buying

You may be willing to spend more money to buy the features that you need. Many functional components of an automobile are well worth an extra charge (such as antilock brakes). However, manufacturers have bundled many of these desirable elements with elements that are pure luxury (leather seats, for example) so you are forced to buy things you do not want in order to get the ones that are valuable and important to you.

The initial cost of a car is, of course, only part of the lifetime cost. The best way to comparison shop for a car is to examine the total expenses for the expected life of the car. Factored into the analysis should be depreciation, miles driven, fuel, maintenance, taxes, and automobile insurance as well as interest on any loan.

Many have found that the cheapest way to own a car is to buy a three-year-old quality used car with low mileage and keep it for a long time. The price of the car used will likely be 50 percent or less of car's sticker price when it was new, since depreciation is highest in the first years. Used cars certified by dealers often have even longer warranties than the dealers' new cars.

Many publications go into great detail on smart car-buying practices, and the advice in *Consumer Reports (CR)* is among the best unbiased advice you can get on buying automobiles and most anything else. A subscription will save you many times its cost if you consult *CR* consistently as a buying guide.

Your Home

Buying a house is likely to be the biggest purchase you will ever make. As with other purchases, functional values and emotional ones are mixed into the decision. For example, you need a home in a certain location to live close to your place of employment—that is a functional requirement. You want to live in a posh part of town for the status value of the location—a psychological requirement.

The recent history of real estate speculation has taught some painful lessons. The idea of buying the most house you could get a loan for time after time (with the least amount of down payment) with an artificially low initial-rate loan on the assumption that the house will appreciate a lot to be sold for a profit has proven to be a fool's game. Such speculative behavior is gambling pure and simple, with a tragic outcome for many caught up in the frenzy.

Food and Groceries

Food expenses vary from a low of buying in bulk quantities and making things from scratch to a high of gourmet meals in fancy restaurants—and everything in-between. The range from pure functional value to pure psychological value is broad, to say nothing about the food's quality and taste.

At one end of the continuum are the basic functional values of food: health and nutrition. Convenience is another functional value for which most are willing to pay. Grandma spent all day in the kitchen baking bread, canning vegetables, making soup, and peeling and mashing potatoes. Today our life styles are different, and we are unwilling or unable to return to those days.

Controlling Impulse Spending

All categories of your spending should be analyzed for opportunities to save. Understanding what you really want and are willing to pay for is the starting point for building your personal spending strategy. We could list scores of things that you need to consider when you spend, but two questions are central:

- Is this really something I want (or need)?

- Can I afford it?

Controlling impulse spending is a two-part process:

1. *Set goals.* Vow never to buy anything significant unless you have money set aside to pay cash for it right now and it is on your goals list. (The exception is that you can use your "walking around money" to buy what you want if you have enough walking around money to cover the purchase.) If something you want to buy is not on the list, why isn't it? What suddenly made the purchase important? What do you want to take off of the list and replace with your new must-have purchase?

2. Even with your discretionary money, *ask yourself these questions at the point of purchase:*

   - Have I planned to buy this? Is it on my list of goals?

   - Will buying this use money I have planned for something else?

   - Have I shopped for the best value?

   - Do I have the cash to pay for it?

   - Do I have to buy it now?

   - What will happen if I wait?

Myth   I have to make the decision to buy this immediately or I will lose the opportunity forever.

Fact   "This is a limited time offer," "you must decide
today," "only three left," and the like are sales
pressure techniques to rush you into a decision
before you are ready. They play on your emotional fear of losing something of value.

Solution   Practice saying "No!" Be especially wary of arti-
ficial timelines for making a decision. Purchase
decisions are better made with time to reflect.

20 Quick Tips for Smart Spending

1. Read about smart shopping practices. There are hundreds of articles
    on how to live better for less and how to get the most for your dol-
    lars and avoid impulse purchasing. Read them regularly to educate
    yourself and learn from the experiences of others.

2. If you are tempted to buy something on impulse, take the item to the
    checkout counter and ask the clerk to hold it for 20 minutes. Then
    walk away from the store for at least 10 minutes. If after 10 minutes
    you still want the item, you will have to walk back. Chances are you
    will change your mind.

3. Take a friend shopping and ask the friend to remind you that you
    had not planned to buy today.

4. Shop, shop, and shop some more before you make a final purchase
    decision. Learn everything you can about the products you intend
    to buy. Taking time to make a shopping decision will slow down
    the process and allow you to solidify the values you are looking for
    and the cost of each item. Such preliminary research will eliminate

buyer's remorse when you finally do make the purchase. A deliberate approach is especially helpful for big-ticket items like television sets, which cost quite a bit and that you expect to have and use for a long time.

5. Pay cash. Give yourself an allowance for a certain time period and put it in cash in your wallet in $20 or $50 bills. If you can only spend cash, the mere process of spending forces you to check how much is in your wallet and how long it has to last. Discipline is built in when you know that what you have must last until the next cash draw.

6. Leave your credit cards at home. Research has shown conclusively that consumers spend significantly more when paying by credit card than when they pay by cash. A credit card has no built-in inhibitors that keep you from spending more than you know you should. Temptation is best controlled by avoidance. If your card is not with you, you are not tempted to use it. As a result, in future the amount of your monthly bill will no longer be a surprise when your monthly credit card bill arrives.

7. If you have a credit card, make sure it is a no-annual-fee card and, after getting rid of your debt, always pay your balance in full every month.

8. Bargain. In some cultures bargaining is expected. In the United States, we expect to bargain when we buy some things, like cars and homes. But it is also true that many stores—particularly small ones where the store owner may be present—are willing to discount prices rather than lose a sale completely. Here are some inoffensive bargaining lines: "I hadn't planned to spend that much." "Does this ever go on sale?" "Let me think about it." "My budget is only _____. What do you have in that price range?" Often you will get a better price or some added value by pursuing such a gambit.

9. Use coupons and take advantage of special sales for things you plan to buy. (However, avoid buying something you had not planned to buy just because there is a coupon or sale.)

10. Learn how to say "No" without feeling guilty. When friends suggest an expensive dinner out, it is okay and appropriate to say something like, "We'd love to join you, but it's not in our budget this month."

Also, don't be afraid to say "No" to a salesperson. Salespeople use highly refined techniques to make you feel inferior if you do not buy their expensive propositions. Do not be embarrassed into making bad financial choices.

11. Buy at the end of a season. Christmas cards are very cheap in January. (Christmas trees are also cheap, but only the fake ones keep.)

12. Join a warehouse club, but avoid buying things on impulse that you did not plan to buy. If you do not need something, any price is too high.

13. Always have a shopping list when going to the grocery store, and do not go when you are hungry and everything is tempting.

14. Always pay on time. Take discounts where they are available and avoid late fees.

15. Arrange for companies to debit your bank directly. Here is how I saved $180 a year. I have three insurance policies with the same company: an automobile policy, a homeowner's policy, and an umbrella liability policy. Originally each policy was billed separately, twice a year, but the insurance company offered the option to divide the yearly amount into 12 installments, for a $5 service fee each month (or $15 total service fee per month for the three accounts when each was paid on the installment plan; $180 per year in fees). I telephoned and the company agreed to consolidate the three bills into one; divide the total bill into 12 payments; and debit the month's payment from the bank. The company waived its service fee when the payment was debited directly from the bank, and I was saved $180 in fees and avoided the trouble of paying the bills every month.

16. If your bank requires minimum balances to waive service charges, maintain those balances. For example, a $16 monthly service charge may be waived with a minimum $1,000 balance. That is a real bargain. Twelve months' service charges equal $192, and if that is waived, it represents 19.2 percent interest on your $1,000.

If you maintain the $1,000 balance and by some lapse write a check that would have overdrawn your account without the $1,000, that $1,000 cushion will save you an overdraft fee (as much as $35). Of course, for that month you'll incur the $16 service charge, but that's still cheaper than a $35 overdraft fee.

17. Look for free sources of recreation. Libraries, museums, parks, and fairs are often free or very inexpensive and are excellent ways to stretch your recreation dollars.

18. Volunteer. Time you spend serving others is time you will not be spending money on yourself and provides real satisfaction.

19. Barter. Trade something you have with someone in exchange for something they have. I have trees and firewood that I exchange for pet sitting and help with yard work.

20. Review your insurance policies. Increasing your deductibles can result in large savings.

Now challenge yourself to add five more tips to this list to stretch your money.

Getting control of all spending in your life is an important goal. Contentment is a state of mind. Look at all of the joys that you have in your life and do not be lured into thinking *what* you have is important to your self-worth.

Take pride in developing smart buying habits and be sure to factor in rewards when you achieve milestone goals.

>> *All About Diamonds* <<

A diamond is an example of a product that has little or no functional component but that has an enormous psychological value. Diamonds are also a special example of an extraordinarily long-range marketing campaign that undertook to do nothing less than successfully shape our culture.

This marketing campaign took as its premise the notion that the measure of a man's love for his mate is proportionate to the size of the diamonds he gives her. A corollary marketing theme has been that this love needs to be demonstrated time and again on anniversaries, birthdays, and holidays.

The most telling proof of the impact of this very effective campaign is the popularization of the diamond industry's slogan, "A Diamond Is Forever." This slogan was designed both to encourage the purchase of new diamonds and to stifle any thought of selling cherished heirloom stones. One should feel guilty if the thought even enters one's mind. Not coincidentally, the highly controlled diamond mining industry wants to discourage any market for used diamonds. It is estimated that several hundred million carets' worth of diamonds are in people's possession, which is many, many times the annual production of diamond mines. An active resale system would compete disastrously with the producers of new diamonds.

In his fascinating 1982 book, *The Rise and Fall of Diamonds: The Shattering of a Brilliant Illusion*, Edward Jay Epstein revealed the origin of the slogan and the rationale of the whole diamond marketing scheme.

In the 1940s, the famous diamond firm DeBeers needed a slogan for selling diamonds that expressed the themes of romance and of legitimacy. In 1948, an N. W. Ayer copywriter came up with "A Diamond Is Forever," which was scrawled on the bottom of a picture of two young lovers on a honeymoon. Even though diamonds can in fact be shattered, chipped, discolored, or incinerated, the concept of eternity perfectly captured the magical qualities that the advertising agency wanted to impute to diamonds. Within a year, "A Diamond Is Forever" became the official slogan of DeBeers.

Buy diamonds if you like and do enjoy them, but do not confuse them with investments that can be resold. As Paul Harvey, the radio host, used to say, "And now you know the rest of the story."

CHAPTER NINE

Credit Cards and Debit Cards

The History of Credit Cards

Credit cards have their origins in the 1920s, when individual companies issued cards to their customers to make buying easier and to create loyalty. Every major gasoline company had its own card, as did most major department stores. In 1950, Diners Club introduced what became known as the Travel and Entertainment card, popularly called T&E cards. American Express introduced its T&E card in 1958. These were not credit cards; they were "charge" cards. The bills had to be paid in full every month. And very few merchants accepted these cards except for restaurants, hotels, and car rental agencies.

Cardholders paid an annual fee to obtain the card, which was honored only at merchant locations that had signed up to honor the card. Merchants would turn in the receipts from the customers and be reimbursed by the card issuer, less a fee that could be several percentage points. The card companies were making money from both the cardholders and the merchants.

A significant change occurred in 1956, when the BankAmericard was introduced in California. For the first time, a cardholder was given the option of not having to pay the amount of charges in full every month. The cardholder had a bank line of credit that could be paid off over a longer period of time. This option marked the beginning of the end for individual loans for consumer purchases of major items such as appliances. Purchasing power (credit) was ready whenever one wanted to purchase on impulse.

In 1966 Bank of America began licensing the card in other states to other banks. Bank of America had to license to other banks because no banks operated in more than one state at that time. In 1976, BankAmericard's name was changed to Visa. Many local and regional banks had their own proprietary cards, which were rarely accepted outside of their own banking locations. Ultimately these banks joined together and formed MasterCard. These two brands now dominate the credit card business.

Acceptance of the retail credit card was slow in coming. Merchants resisted paying a fee from their sales to the retail cards and preferred their own "in-house" credit departments. This attitude was prevalent even though the evidence was clear that the cost of running an in-house credit operation coupled with the inevitable accounts that failed to pay was more costly than the fees to the bank-run retail cards. Eventually the evidence became overwhelming, and many merchants ceased extending credit directly to their customers.

Extensive research revealed that resistance from potential cardholders was twofold. First, people were afraid that someone might somehow get access to their cards and charge things to them. What would happen to the cardholders in that case and how could they be protected? This barrier to acceptance was easily addressed by guaranteeing a limit of liability to the cardholder for fraudulent use.

Second, cardholders had a deep-seated fear that they themselves would misuse the cards. No easy answer to this fear has ever been found. Instead, banks aggressively solicited merchants to agree to accept their cards, and simultaneously the banks did massive mailings of cards to individuals, with significant incentives for using the cards. The fear of misuse by oneself faded into the background as the inarguable benefits of credit and convenience were recognized.

In the 1960s, the upshot of the banks' two-pronged approach was a wave of purchasing by credit-challenged people who simply did not pay their bills. Banks charged off hundreds of millions of dollars of losses while they tried to figure out just who should qualify to have a card. Today, banks are still trying to figure that out.

Credit Cards Today

Personal misuse of credit cards has today reached epidemic proportions. Blame for this misuse is hard to pinpoint. Our culture has embraced as acceptable the notion of being in debt and satisfying our whims immediately instead of postponing our purchases until we have cash in hand. The banks have simultaneously relaxed their standards and have declined to be the monitors of personal profligacy.

Credit card issuers are flooding creditworthy people with preapproved card offers. The card issuers prefer that you charge as much as you can and pay as little as you can, preferably a few days late. If you don't pay your balance or pay late, the issuers earn exorbitant interest rates and obscene late fees and penalties. Since you are a source of income for the card issuers, do not expect to hear admonitions about self-control and restraint from them. It is up to you to resist the sales pitches.

This brings us to you. How are you managing your credit card debt? If you are out of control, increasing balances, reaching credit limits, or making only minimum or late payments, it is time to take drastic steps.

Some counselors and debt advisors have an absolute approach. Pay off all of your credit card debt, never ever charge anything again, and destroy your cards. This approach is drastic but it will work. I am reluctant to suggest otherwise, except that in reality there are some benefits to using a credit card. I will discuss those later in this chapter. But the drastic approach misses the root of the problem.

Having a credit card does not cause you to be in debt any more than having dishes causes you to get fat. (A "break all the dishes" diet might actually work, however.) What is needed is the discipline to manage how you spend money and to live within your means. You and only you are accountable for your circumstances. Do not blame the credit card issuers for your failings. As recommended in Chapter 8, "Spending Strategies," learn to say NO.

Your first line of defense against excess spending is to have goals and a spending system designed to achieve contentment by living within your means.

The problem arises not because of the way (cash, check, or plastic) in which you purchase anything, but rather because of what you purchase and when.

On the one hand, if you use a credit card as a convenience for programmed expenses and have cash allocated to pay the credit card bill in full every month, the credit card is a marvelous convenience. And, as we will see, there are times both when the credit card purchase adds special benefits and when a credit card is the only practical method of payment.

On the other hand, using a credit card to buy things sooner than you are prepared to pay for them is foolish. Instant gratification instead of delayed gratification is a bad habit. Save up for what you want to buy. Credit card debt is extraordinarily expensive.

A credit card is useful as short-term "credit," and that "credit" is free if you pay the balance in full every month (and have a "no annual fee" card). A credit card is a very expensive way to get long-term "financing."

Since this book is about giving yourself a raise, money you do not have to pay to someone else is money in your pocket. Even a nominal interest rate uses your money in a "no value to you" way. In fact, since credit card interest rates are among the highest charged for anything, your obvious plan should be to avoid credit card debt entirely.

Credit Card Benefits

Credit cards are bundled with a wide array of free benefits that may be worthwhile. Read your card documents to understand the ones you may have. The following is a partial list.

1. **Extended Warranties:** If you purchase a product using the card, the purchase may extend the warranty of the product beyond the warranty that comes with the product. Some credit cards even cover theft of the product or accidental damage to the product for some period of time.

2. **Rental Car Insurance:** Renting a car exposes you to risk if the car is damaged but you may not need to buy insurance from the car rental company. Your own automobile insurance policy may cover insurance risks on a rental car, and most credit cards provide automatic free coverage for rental cars if the rental is charged to the card. The terms vary but could save you a lot of money on car rentals.

3. **Ease of Return:** Purchases made on a credit card are simple to return for credit. If you buy from catalogs or on the Internet, a credit card is the simplest way to pay and assures you can return something that is not what you expected, is defective, or is the wrong size.

4. **Limited Risk for Loss or Misuse:** If your card is lost or stolen and the loss or theft is reported as required by the card terms, your liability is limited to $50. In practice, even the $50 is rarely assessed.

5. **Acceptance:** Major credit cards are accepted almost everywhere around the world. In a real crunch you can get a cash advance at most banks, both your own and others. Cash advances are expensive, however, because of various fees and interest assessed if you do not pay them on the next billing.

6. **Rewards:** Many cards now have some sort of a reward program based on the total dollar value of your purchases. Be careful. Sometimes the value of the rewards is offset by other card costs such as an annual fee. Be certain the rewards are really of value to you.

7. **Records:** Monthly statements are useful for tracking your spending habits. Some cards provide a year-end summary statement sorted by category with subtotals.

Credit Card Risks

Lost or Stolen Card

Even if you do not end up paying for misuse when you lose a card or your card is stolen, the hassle of reporting the loss, identifying the charges that are not yours, and getting a duplicate card can be time consuming. Credit cards are one of the easiest ways for someone to steal your identity.

Overspending

A credit card makes it easy to spend money you do not have.

Practical Tips

The following is a list of practical tips for the use of credit cards:

- Obtain a credit card that does not charge an annual fee.

- When you use your card, be sure to get the card back. Be cautious when your card disappears and then comes back to be signed (as in most restaurants.) Is it your card? Is the amount on the bill and on the slip you are signing the same?

- Open your credit card statements immediately. If you are using electronic banking, you can pay the bill right away, marked for a delivery date that should be three or four days before the due date. This procedure will avoid late fees and interest charges (if you pay the entire balance of the bill).

- Keep your charge slips, and when you open your statement, check each of the charge slips against entries on the statement. It is very common for charges to grow mysteriously to more than you authorized for the charge slip that you signed, particularly in restaurants, where tips may increase by magic.

- Report discrepancies immediately and explicitly follow the rules given to you by your card issuer. Do not pay for disputed amounts. If you pay a disputed amount, you may waive your right to recover the disputed amount.

- Never pay late. Never! Late payment is the fastest way to wreck your credit and accrue fees.

- Read all of the rules and disclosures, because you are responsible for them. Even though the type may be very small, most of the language is easy to understand.

- Do not use the teaser checks (just another type of cash advance) the credit card issuer sends you. Shred them.

- Shred unsolicited card offers.

- Sign your card immediately upon receipt.

- Understand the rewards program if your card has one.

- Make a photocopy of everything in your wallet. Spread out your credit cards, driver's license, insurance cards, and anything else you carry in your wallet on a copy machine. Copy both sides. Then make a list of each account and the telephone number to call to report a lost card. Make several copies of the list and put them in a convenient place, such as inside the telephone directory or at your desk. Then, if you have the misfortune of having your wallet stolen or you lose your wallet, you can make the required calls quickly.

Debit Cards

If you have an ATM card, you have a limited-use debit card. Most ATM cards issued now are general-purpose debit cards that can be used as cash withdrawal cards at ATM machines and for purchases. A debit card subtracts money directly and immediately from the bank account to which it is linked. You pay as you use it. No separate statement arrives at the end of the month for payment. The transactions appear on your monthly bank statement.

Two different methods for processing purchases by debit card are common, depending on the service the merchant uses. You may be asked to swipe your card through a terminal at the point of purchase and enter a pin number, or the merchant may imprint your card on a paper receipt that you sign. The transaction processes resemble those used for a credit card, but the money comes out of your deposit account immediately.

Debit Card Risks

A debit card may pose a much greater risk than that posed by a credit card. The limit of your liability for fraudulent purchases on debit cards varies and may not be protected by federal statute in the same way your credit card liability is. Therefore a lost or stolen debit card is very serious.

If, for example, your card is stolen and is used to make a purchase, your bank account is charged immediately. If your balance is thus lowered and checks you have written arrive at the bank for payment, an "insufficient funds" situation may result and checks will be bounced, causing embarrassment and possible fees. The bank may assess a fee, of course, and the payee to whom the check was written may also assess a fee. A misused debit card can clean out your bank account before you even know about it. The bank may or may not reimburse you for these fraudulent charges, and even if the bank does reimburse, the reimbursement process may take some time. Meanwhile you are inconvenienced.

If you have linked your bank accounts to provide overdraft protection, a misused debit card can access every account linked to it, possibly including your credit card accounts.

At the time of this writing, there is much pressure to change the laws to extend more protection to consumers. Even if the laws are expanded to provide you more protection, the time and inconvenience of fixing a problem can be awful. Be cautious with your plastic!

Another feature related to debit cards that surprises many people is the practice of "blocking" used by merchants accepting debit cards. Let's use renting a car as an example. If you have a *credit card*, the car rental agency accepts the credit card as evidence you are able to pay for the rental of the car. A debit card carries no such assurance, so the rental company contacts the issuing bank and asks that the potential amount of your rental fee be blocked in advance. The rental company does not tell you that it just blocked $500 to cover the one-week rental of a car on your vacation. That block will not be released until you return the car and settle up with the rental company. Blocking can cause you some real surprises.

Rule: Be very very careful with your debit card.

Tips

If you are using a bank account to obtain an ATM or debit card only for personal "walking around money," do not expose your primary checking account to the risk of a debit card loss by linking the accounts.

Do not use ATM machines that charge a fee for cash withdrawals. If you need cash, get it from your own bank's ATM. Or, if you use the debit card for a purchase, ask for cash back.

More Information

Credit cards and debit cards are important parts of our everyday lives. The more you know about each of them beyond the brief discussion in this chapter, the safer you will be from fraud, misuse, or identity theft.

A nonprofit organization, the Privacy Rights Clearing House, has some of the most readable, practical, and thorough reports to be found, and they can be downloaded free from its Web site. The following is a must-read report: *Fact Sheet 32: Paper or Plastic: What Have You Got to Lose?* (http://www.privacyrights.org/fs/fs32-paperplastic.htm).

Another resource is the exhaustive Web site for understanding nearly anything, "How Stuff Works." If you want to know what time it is, look at a watch. If you want to know how to build a watch, you need more information than just how to tell time. "How Stuff Works" is where to go. This report is definitely worth reading: *How Credit Cards Work* (http://money.howstuffworks.com/credit-card.htm/printable).

Summary

Credit and debit cards are marvels of our electronic banking world. If you use them appropriately, they are great conveniences. If you misuse them, they have the potential to seriously damage your life. The choice is yours.

≫≫ *Before Credit Cards* ≪≪

Before the establishment of the credit card as we know it today, consumers financing major purchases faced a tortuous process. Merchants would sell an item (let's say a refrigerator) on a "time plan." The customer would complete an exhaustive questionnaire that the merchant would submit to its bank for approval. If the bank approved the loan, the bank would fund the purchase by paying the merchant and would issue a coupon book to the buyer for making monthly payments.

These loans were referred to as "recourse paper." The merchant guaranteed to the bank that the buyer would pay back the loan. If the loan was not repaid as agreed, the bank charged back the loan to the merchant, who then likely as not repossessed the item to try to recover the loss.

In those days, the criteria for getting credit were very straightforward. (1) Did you have the ability to repay the loan? This ability to repay was determined by comparing your income to your expenses to see if enough money was left over to make the payments. (2) Did you have the willingness to repay the loan? A willingness to repay was determined by your credit history. Today, your credit score incorporates a similar creditworthiness analysis.

Recourse lending is still common in the automobile industry. People with weak credit can still buy and finance a car because they are literally borrowing the money from the dealer. Interest rates for such loans may be high, but you can buy a car in this manner.

PART TWO

Financial Literacy 101

**AN INTRODUCTION TO THINGS
YOU REALLY NEED TO KNOW**

Overview

Part 2 is a series of simple introductions to subjects that have great impact on your financial life and peace of mind. Each subject is vast and the topic of many books. In fact, so much has been written about each subject that just deciding where to start learning about the topic can be overwhelming and more than a little confusing. It is beyond the scope of this book to do any more than familiarize you with the topics and get you started on the road to more comprehensive study.

These chapters are starting points to demystify topics that can at times be intimidating. For example, pick up any book on investing for the first time and chances are that you will be surprised by the sheer magnitude of the subject matter. So where do you begin without becoming discouraged?

The simple truth is you can either learn about these topics yourself or be forever vulnerable to having someone make bad decisions on your behalf, decisions that you ultimately pay for. What happens to you in your financial life is strictly up to you.

The chapters in Part 2 will introduce you to the following essential financial topics:

- Chapter 10: Investing and Retirement

- Chapter 11: Understanding Risk

- Chapter 12: Government Programs

- Chapter 13: Insurance

- Chapter 14: Credit Scores and Identity Theft

- Chapter 15: Emergency Preparedness

- Chapter 16: The Secrets of Making Lots of Money

- Chapter 17: Five Secrets of Success

With this foundation you are encouraged to continue learning how each topic impacts your financial life.

CHAPTER TEN

Retirement and Investing

In Part 1 of this book, I focused on setting goals, developing a spending plan, and getting out of debt. The next step is planning for your future. However, I should first reiterate that *Give Yourself a RAISE* is not a book devoted to exhaustive investing/retirement strategies. Unlimited resources already exist on those subjects. Rather, the following discussion on investing and retirement is meant to be a starting point.

An essential part of your financial literacy is to become aware of the magnitude of the retirement issues facing you so that you can begin planning now for the future. Retirement will arrive faster than you expect.

Today, you earn a paycheck for the time you work. When you retire, the paycheck stops, along with anything else your employer was paying for, such as health insurance. What also stops is that raise you got from time to time. Think back to what you were earning 10 or 20 years ago. Could you live comfortably today on that amount? People retiring today can realistically expect to live for more than 20 years. What will prices for everyday items be then?

How Much Do You Need in Retirement?

"You working for money" has to be replaced by "money working for you." The question is, "How much do I need to replace my paycheck?" Table 10.1

Table 10.1   Investment Required at the Time of Retirement to Replace Annual Pay
(assumes principal not withdrawn)

Current Wage Rate		Investment Required at Time of Retirement to Replace Annual Pay (Percentage Rates of Return on Investment at Time of Retirement)						
Hourly pay	Annual gross	2 percent	3 percent	4 percent	5 percent	6 percent	8 percent	10 percent
$10.00	$20,800	$1,040,000	$693,333	$520,000	$416,000	$346,667	$260,000	$208,000
$15.00	$31,200	$1,560,000	$1,040,000	$780,000	$624,000	$520,000	$390,000	$312,000
$20.00	$41,600	$2,080,000	$1,386,667	$1,040,000	$832,000	$693,333	$520,000	$416,000
$25.00	$52,000	$2,600,000	$1,733,333	$1,300,000	$1,040,000	$866,667	$650,000	$520,000
$30.00	$62,400	$3,120,000	$2,080,000	$1,560,000	$1,248,000	$1,040,000	$780,000	$624,000

is a quick calculation of simple dollar-for-dollar replacement (how much you need in savings, earning what rate of return, to replace your paycheck).

On the left in Table 10.1 is an hourly wage rate extended to an annual equivalent, assuming 2,080 normal paid hours per year. Across the top of the table are seven percentage rates of return on investment (from 2 percent to 10 percent). Locate your hourly wage rate and go across to the column that has the average rate you think your investments can return in the future. In the box is the amount of cash that needs to be working for you (invested for you at that rate of return) simply to replace your paycheck.

For example, if you make $10 per hour ($20,800 per year) and you think that when you retire you will be able to obtain a 4 percent rate of return on retirement investments, you will need to have accumulated $520,000 by the time you retire to replace your $20,800 pay.

To save $520,000, you have to save about $350 a month now, earning 8 percent (an unrealistically high return rate at this writing) for 30 years. This means that you have to be setting aside about 14 hours' pay every month, and it will need to be earning 8 percent interest. That is, you need to be setting aside about 8 percent of your gross pay *if you have 30 years to reach your goal.* Now you know why it is important to automatically save at least 10 percent of your gross pay every paycheck. Paying yourself first really matters.

If you start this program 10 years earlier and *have 40 years to reach your goal,* you can reach the same $520,000 by setting aside only $150 a month, earning 8 percent interest. If you wait until you *have only 20 years to reach your goal,* you will need to set aside $880 a month earning 8 percent.

Note that these sample calculations all assume earning a steady 8 percent, and that is very high at the time of this writing. A rate of return of 5 percent with safety is still high but more realistic. If 5 percent is used, the 30-year monthly savings would be $625 to reach $520,000.

This model assumes that in retirement you will not be withdrawing any of the principal from your savings but will simply be using the flow of interest from it. If you withdraw principal systematically over time, you could have more to live on, but of course you cannot predict how long you will live, so you may run out of money.

Most people will have additional sources of retirement income such as Social Security benefits. The preceding discussion is merely to show you how much it would take to replace your paycheck if for the sake of argument interest from investments was your only source of retirement income.

These are very simple examples with very limited assumptions. Your own situation will be different, and that is reason to consult with a professional financial advisor to assess your own situation. Three things are clear: (1) You need to be setting aside a lot of money to maintain your life style after you retire, (2) the sooner you start saving, the easier it will be because time is on your side, and (3) future interest rates are anybody's guess. You need to plan for the worst-case scenarios and be realistic about your expectations.

Where Is the Money Coming From?

Retirement planning requires identifying potential sources of income and making assumptions about the future. The fact that nobody can predict the future makes the exercise fraught with risk, but nonetheless you must tackle the task sooner rather than later.

Money can come from:

- Savings

- Investments

- Interest earned

- Dividends

- Pensions

- Social Security

- Inheritances and gifts

- Future pay increases

- Part-time work

- Winning the lottery

Myth My stockbroker and insurance agent offer free financial advice and estate planning.

Fact There is no free lunch. Be especially cautious of financial advice for which you do not pay. It is impossible for a person who earns a "commission" from a product or service sold to you to be unbiased about that product. Free estate planning is a tool for the planner to sell you something. Note that there is nothing inherently wrong about this and the advice may in fact be valuable. However, you need to know that such advice comes with a bias.

Solution "How do you get paid?" is always the first question to ask advisors. Be certain that the advisors' plans are right for you, not for them.

The Power of Compound Interest

Money that you save now will grow over time if it is allowed to "compound." Compounding means that you allow the earnings of investments to be reinvested in the principal instead of being paid to you. Each dollar saved earns a certain percentage in interest. If that interest payment is left with the original saving, there is more principal earning interest in the next period. Two variables affect compounding: (1) the interest rate that is paid and (2) the time for which the money is invested. The power of time is illustrated in the following example.

If you invest $1,000 at an annual return of 5 percent, it will be worth $1,050 at the end of one year. At the end of three years, if you leave the earnings with the principal, the original $1,000 will have compounded to $1,161.47. Leave it invested for 10 years, $1,647.01; 20 years, $2,712.64;

25 years, $3,481.29; 30 years, $4,467.74, and 40 years, $7,358.42. (These figures are based on monthly compounding.)

Calculations can be made with any set of assumptions about (1) the amount of money to be saved each time period, (2) the number of time periods (usually years), and (3) the target amount required. With any two numbers you can solve for the other one. Many retirement-planning Web sites have a program into which you can simply enter your numbers.

The Rule of 72

The Rule of 72 is often used as a simple example of the relationship between interest rates and the result of compounding. The Rule of 72 gives you the time it takes to double your money given a known rate of interest.

Rule: Divide 72 by the interest rate to get the time it will take for your money to double. The following are some examples of the Rule of 72 applied a range of interest rates.

Interest Rate of Return	Years Invested to Double Money
2 percent	72/2 = 36 years
3 percent	72/3 = 24 years
5 percent	72/5 = 14.4 years
8 percent	72/8 = 9 years
12 percent	72/12 = 6 years

The longer you wait to start investing, the more you will need to set aside to reach your goals because the power of compounding has not been working for you. The lower the interest rates you earn, the longer it will take to reach your goals.

Unfortunately, most people do not have the luxury of 40 years to invest their money before they need the money. If you assume that you will retire at age 65, ideally you would need to start a serious systematic program of setting aside money by the time you are 25 years old (on the premise of investing over a 40-year period). Most people at that age have growing expenses and lower income and put off saving.

By the way, the power of compounding works against you when you have debt. If you have credit card balances that have an interest rate of 18 percent and carry a balance, the card issuer is doubling his money in 4 years! The refrigerator you thought you bought for $1,500 could cost you double that amount if you make only minimum payments. This is why a key premise of this book is to get out of debt and stay out of debt.

Expenses When Retired

What about your expenses when you retire? Will they go up or down or stay the same? Some will go down. Social Security contributions now being withheld from your gross pay will end when you stop working. That adds about 6 percent to the amount of your net after-tax paycheck.

Some expenses, such as health care, can be expected to go up, because in retirement your employer will probably cease paying a portion of the cost of your insurance. It is anyone's guess what medical benefits will be paid by the government by the time you retire. Recreation and travel expenditures may go up as you start a retirement life style. You need to plan each category of present expenses and estimate how the expense will change when you retire, not just in the first year but as you age.

Those best prepared to retire are those with no debt and a big chunk of savings and those who are living well within their means. Without house payments, car payments, tuition payments for the kids in college, or credit card debt, you will have the maximum choices of how you will live with whatever money you have coming in.

In a later section I will explain "risk," because one of your concerns is to make sure the money you set aside for the future is there when you need it. The biggest risk takers are gamblers, and gamblers have a history of dying broke without meaning to.

About Investments

What Is an Investment?

An investment is money (capital) put to work with the expectation that it will be more valuable in the future. Value can increase by the investment either becoming more valuable over time (like a stock) or producing a stream of earnings from time to time, such as interest or dividends.

Investments have two basic forms:

1. Debt investments

2. Equity investments

Debt Investments

A debt investment is money you lend to someone from which you earn interest, and ultimately you are repaid. A certificate of deposit (CD) at a bank is money you lend to the bank for a certain period that the bank may in turn lend to others. You receive interest and get back all of your money when the CD matures. Bonds issued by governments or corporations are also debt instruments. The interest you receive on such bonds is a constant amount and is determined when the instruments are created.

Myth   The experts can reliably identify riskless extraordinary opportunities.

Fact   If it seems too good to be true, it probably is. Every illusion rests on a plausibility. Con artists do not go around in black capes carrying concealed daggers. They carry attaché cases, wear expensive suits, and seem so knowledgeable and trustworthy.

Solution   Just trusting the experts is risky. Take the time to learn about your choices. Resources for doing so are plentiful. Do not be in a hurry to risk what you cannot afford to lose. Never invest in anything you do not understand completely! "Oh by the way" is not a welcome phrase when something turns out to be different from what you thought.

For example, a five-year 5 percent $5,000 CD will pay you $250 every year for five years. You may receive that interest as income or allow the interest to stay in the CD and compound—that is, each interest payment is reinvested in the CD and earns the same rate of return. Assuming you allowed your annual interest payments to compound, your original investment will be worth $6,381 at the end of five years.

Equity Investments

Equity is ownership. A share of stock in a company is part ownership of the company. When you buy stock, most often you will be buying from another shareholder rather than being an original investor buying directly from the company. (Stocks in a publicly held company are sold by stockbrokers who match up buyers or sellers.) You make money if in the future somebody wants to pay you more for the stock than you paid for it or if the company pays a dividend from its earnings.

When you sell the stock, you may get less for the stock than you paid for it if the company has not performed well.

To build an investment portfolio you may select several different investments, in both stocks and bonds, to diversify. The term *diversification* refers to spreading your risk by choosing a variety of investments instead of investing in a few things or in just one thing.

Mutual Funds

Mutual funds are collections of investments put together by mutual fund companies. Instead of buying individual stocks (or bonds), you buy a share of the mutual fund. These shares can be bought and sold just like individual investments. Each fund produces a prospectus that explains the fund and its investment philosophy.

Getting Started

Many books are available on investing for beginners, and as you accumulate enough money to become an investor, it is important that you read, learn, and understand what you are buying.

Characteristics of Investments

Every investment has a combination of these three factors:

1. Risk versus safety

2. Return (or yield)

3. Liquidity (how quickly an investment can be turned into cash)

Typically these factors are related. (There are occasional exceptions.) For all intents and purposes you may assume that you can get two of the three factors in your favor but not all three. For example, if an investment is promoted as being very low risk and very high liquidity, it is likely also very low yield. High yields come from poor liquidity or high risk or both.

1. Risk Versus Safety

At one end of the "risk/safety" scale, safety is very high and risk is very low. U.S. government bonds are at this end; they are assumed to be riskless. That is, you will always get your money back when the bond matures.

Lending your irresponsible cousin money to start a business is probably at the high-risk/low-safety end of the scale. Chapter 11 discusses risk in more detail.

2. Return (or Yield)

As you might expect, the return (or yield or interest) you receive goes up as the risk goes up. Conversely, as the risk goes down, the yield is likely to be less. If you are presented with an opportunity to earn a high yield, you may rationally expect that you are taking on more risk.

Keep these two truths in mind at all times when you are making investments: (1) There is no free lunch, and (2) if it seems too good to be true, it probably is. People have lost their entire fortunes by ignoring these rules of the road.

3. Liquidity

Liquidity describes how easily and quickly an investment can be turned into cash, and it is the third element of investments. Savings accounts and publicly traded stocks and bonds are examples of highly liquid investments. The bank will give you back your money from a savings account immediately, and a stockbroker can sell your stocks/bonds and get cash to you in a few days because there is a formal market to facilitate the buying and selling of securities.

Yield on high-liquidity investments typically is low. As the time it takes to turn an investment into cash lengthens, investors want a higher yield for giving up ready access to their money. This higher yield is called "the liquidity premium." In normal circumstances, long-term bonds or long-term bank CDs pay more than the short-term bonds or CDs. This difference is called the "yield curve" and represents the premium required for loss of liquidity.

Undeveloped land in the desert is an example of a very-low-liquidity investment. Low demand for such land and the absence of a formal trading market make turning the land into cash difficult.

Measures of Value

No discussion of investing would be complete without at least a cursory look at the concept of "value," or what something is worth.

Cost

"Cost" is one way to measure value. "Original cost" is what you paid for something. But as we know, some things—like automobiles—quickly become less valuable than what we paid for them; that is, they depreciate.

Replacement Cost

"Replacement cost" is another way to measure value. A house you bought 20 years ago probably could not be replaced today for the same price you originally paid. So you see the value of your house as having appreciated, or grown in value.

Market Value

"Market value" is the price someone else is willing to pay for something. Market value is the only relevant way to measure the value of anything you plan to sell. What you paid for anything becomes instantly irrelevant. All that matters is what someone is willing to pay for it now. No matter what you think something is worth, or what you paid for it, or what it would take to replace it, its value is *only* what someone is willing to pay for it. If that amount is too low, you may elect not to sell. Your house is a good example.

When you make an investment, you are expecting the future market value to increase.

Stock Prices and Value

What causes stock prices to change?

The value of a stock in the mind of an investor is an estimate (guess) of what it will be worth in the future. Will the company grow and prosper? Will other investors be interested in owning the shares, and at what price?

Suppose a company's stock is selling for $60 a share and that last year the company profits were equivalent to $5 for each share of stock that was outstanding. This information is easy to obtain. This means that the company stock is selling for a price-to-earnings (P/E) ratio of 12 (60/5 = 12). I will skip discussing how much of that is paid out to the shareholders in the form of dividends.

Now suppose the company earnings next year were equivalent to $5.50 a share (a growth of 10 percent). With the same P/E ratio, the stock could be expected to sell for $66 a share. What if the news about the company was very good and there was an expectation that in three years the company's earnings would reach $10 a share? On the same price model, the stock's price could be expected to be $120 a share. How sure the investors are of this growth will obviously have an impact on the price.

So one way a company's stock price increases is from actual or expected earnings growth.

The other factor driving stock prices is investors' assessment of how favored the company or the industry will be. Exuberance for a company or a particular industry (such as the high-tech companies in the 1990s) may lead investors to accept a higher P/E ratio. Suppose the sample company stock above sells for a P/E ratio of 20 instead of 12. With $5 earnings expect a stock price of $100 per share; $5.50 in earnings gives $110 per share; $10 in earnings results in a $200 share price.

The dynamics work the other way, too. Lower earnings and loss of favor cause investors to withdraw and stock prices to fall. There are no guarantees! Predictions about the future are riskier the farther into the future you try to see.

In summary, when you invest, you expect to share in the good fortunes of the future and risk the investment being worth less as well.

Bond Value

Bonds and most debt investments have a different scenario from stocks. Whereas in stock or equity investing you are literally owning a part of the company, in debt investing you are loaning money. Stocks can go up or down. Bond yield is locked in and will never be higher or lower than the interest rate at which the bond was issued.

These features do not mean bonds are without risk, but it is a different kind of risk, credit risk.

"Credit risk" refers to the possibility that the organization to which you are lending money—whether it is a company or a government agency—cannot pay the interest or principal as it becomes due.

"Market risk" is the possibility that you cannot sell the bond before maturity for the same amount that you paid for it. Even with no credit risk and the assurance you will get all of your money back at maturity, the market price may be less depending on current interest rates.

A discussion of bond investing is beyond the scope of this book. Many reference books are available when you are ready to start serious investing.

Summary

Planning for retirement requires an investment of time to learn your choices. Start now.

>> *Sudden Wealth* <<

A sudden, unexpected windfall of a whole bunch of money is something about which we all fantasize but with which few of us are ready to deal when it happens. On a game show one evening, a young woman won several hundred thousand dollars. When asked what she planned to do with her winnings, she replied, "I am going to take a whole lot of my friends on a vacation to Iceland." That's cool! (Pun intended.)

So what would you do? Are you prepared and disciplined enough to make wise choices or will you look back and regret your actions?

Historically, people who "win big" manage to spend most if not all of the money in a very short time. The million-dollar winner of one reality TV show in the end failed to pay federal income taxes and wound up doing jail time.

Large amounts of money (several times greater than an annual income) come from a wide variety of sources other than game shows and lotteries. Inheritances, insurance claim settlements, divorce property distributions, life insurance, and lump sum retirement benefits all are likely sources of a chunk of money.

The first impulse on receiving a windfall is to substantially reward yourself. The second is to generously bestow some of the abundance on loved ones. It is fun and satisfying to give and share.

If you have little or no experience managing large sums of money, you probably will think that your windfall is larger than it really is, that there is plenty to go around, and that it will last forever. Planning to make the windfall last is dull indeed in comparison to the rush of coming into the pot of gold. However, as a one-time event, when the windfall is gone, it is gone forever. It will require self-control to make it last.

If you come into a windfall, I recommend the following:

- The very first thing you should do with sudden wealth is—nothing. Store it safely. Let the thrill subside so that your rational persona can take over from your emotional persona. Do not indulge yourself with a spending spree.

- Store the money for at least six months, or preferably one year, while you develop a plan. Bank CDs are safe and will earn money while you are planning. If your winnings are more than the FDIC will insure at one bank, divide the money among multiple banks to be sure your deposit is fully covered by FDIC insurance. The money market accounts of stock brokerage firms are similarly safe. Spending your money will not be any less satisfying because you waited before spending.

- Learn to say "No," or at least "Not yet," to the inevitable volunteers who offer to help you part company with your newfound affluence.

- Hire a reputable fee-only financial planner to show you investment options and risks. Do not accept advice from anyone who earns a commission selling you something. Such people have a built-in conflict of interest and cannot be unbiased.

- Develop a written plan and stick to it. If it includes rewarding yourself, that's fine. If it includes massive generosity, that is fine, too.

CHAPTER ELEVEN

Understanding Risk

Risk takes many forms in our lives, and we do many things to protect ourselves from the consequences of events that may or may not happen. Each of us has a different tolerance for risk based on our experiences and emotional makeup. What may appear to one person as highly risky may to another person be an ordinary activity. Skydiving and alligator wrestling come to mind.

Understanding risk helps us deal with risk, either by avoiding it or by taking risk-minimization actions. For example, the risk of being in an automobile accident occurs every time we are in a car. To reduce the risk, we practice safe driving, we buy cars with safety features such as antilock brakes, we keep good tires on the car, and finally, we fasten our seatbelts to minimize the risk of injury if we do have an accident. If the roads are icy or we are tired or we have to drive at night in the rain, we may choose not to drive at all.

Assessing risk is very difficult because we are always trying to predict what will happen in the future. No matter how difficult it is, we need to try to assess our exposure to events of the future and take steps to insulate ourselves from damages that may occur.

You yourself are the first and most significant risk. All of us are the sum total of all of our experiences (good and bad), education, emotional makeup, and genetic profile. We are who we are. The better we understand our own strengths and limitations, the better equipped we are to deal with risks presented to us.

Each of us has a level of tolerance for risk ranging from no tolerance to the other extreme of fearlessness. You probably have a pretty good idea where you fall on this scale. Risk occurs when you move outside of your comfort zone and are forced to make decisions with which you are uncomfortable. Some people are afraid to admit what they do not know and are reluctant to seek help, but sometimes we have no choice except to make decisions that are outside our experience. We need to have strategies to protect ourselves when this occurs.

One of the worst things you can do when faced with a risky decision is to pretend that it is something with which you are really comfortable. Most of the time seeking more facts or additional expertise can significantly reduce risk, especially when the decisions you must make are irreversible. An old country saying puts it concisely: "Don't put your foot in a bucket you can't get it out of!"

Since this book is about money in your life, what follows is a simple description of the kinds of risk you will encounter when managing money. All the risks described are about what will happen in the future. We all know how imprecise the weather forecast is for a week away. With money decisions, we are faced with predicting the future years away.

Credit Risk

Credit risk is easy to understand. It is the risk that someone or some organization will not have the money to pay their debts. Lending money to your nephew to start a new business involves the real possibility that the business will not generate enough money to pay you back. That is credit risk in a nutshell.

Government and corporate bonds all have credit risk and have published credit risk ratings. The riskier bonds pay more because that is the only way they can attract investors. U.S. government bonds are assumed to be free of credit risk. This assumption has never been seriously tested in the United States. You can safely assume that you will get back the interest payments and your entire principal *if* you hold the bonds until they mature. If you have to sell them before they mature, you face a different kind of risk—market risk.

Market Risk

Market risk exists because investment value is driven by the existence of willing buyers. If there are no buyers, your investment is worth nothing, which is the ultimate market risk. If buyers for what you are trying to sell are willing only to pay less for the item than you paid for it, you have experienced market risk. A few examples will demonstrate market risk at work.

1. Bonds may be perfectly safe if held to maturity (no credit risk), but if you need to sell them before maturity, buyers may not be willing to pay the full price.

2. Stock prices rising and falling are visible signs of the market at work.

3. Your house is very sensitive to market conditions. If you have to sell your home in a hurry, you may have to reduce your price substantially.

4. Collectibles have very volatile market risk. Trends come and go. Some collectibles have relatively mature markets for buying *and* selling— you need both. Coins, stamps, and baseball cards are collectibles with established markets for both buying and selling. Although some mass-merchandised items like dolls, toys, and china are marketed as collectibles, they may prove very hard to sell and should be bought with the idea that they are solely for current pleasure, not future gain.

Market risk varies over time. You may elect to wait when making a sale until the market is better, but it is impossible to predict when a market for a specific item will improve, if ever.

Supply and demand also drive market risk. Scarce things that people want tend to go up in price. Plentiful things that are easy to acquire drive prices down.

Interest-Rate Risk

Interest-rate risk is encountered when you face interest rate changes that affect you, either in the interest you receive on an investment or the interest you pay on a loan. On the side of interest you receive, if you have a five-year bank CD earning 5 percent and your bank changes its rate so that a new CD for the same term would be priced to yield 6.5 percent, you are stuck with the lower rate until your CD matures. That is investment-interest-rate risk.

On the side of interest that you pay, a variable-rate home mortgage may be set to reprice from its original rate at various times in the future. If you borrowed $250,000 at an introductory rate of 3.5 percent for the first three

Myth	Experts can accurately forecast the future.
Fact	Forecasting is a form of gambling. Economists spend half of their time projecting the future and the other half explaining why the last forecast was wrong. The experts' track records on forecasting are no better than average. Recent reports of top executives at well-known financial firms getting fired after their companies posted multibillion-dollar losses are sad testimony to the "expertise" of these experts. One editorial writer summarized the problem with simply, "They had no idea of the real risks of what they were doing." And by the way—the losses were their clients' money, not their own. Do you want to trust them with your money?
Solution	Your strategy is to be prepared for alternatives and not fixate on "sure things" from someone else's perspective. Recognize that two things are out of your control: (1) things that occurred in the past and (2) what is going to happen in the future. (For example, what is going to happen to interest rates.)

years, your payments would be $1,119.35 per month on a 30-year mortgage. If the interest rate resets to 5.75 percent, your payments would now be $1,451.97; that is $332.62 a month higher. Are you prepared to pay that? This increase may occur at an inconvenient time and disrupt your finances. That is loan interest rate risk.

Purchasing Power Risk

The "risk" of purchasing power is that a dollar today buys less than it did 20 years ago, and a dollar tomorrow can be expected to buy less than it does today. This phenomenon fits the classic definition of inflation. When planning for the future, you must factor in what things will cost in the future; you must factor in inflation. If you stuff your savings in a mattress where it earns no interest, the money actually is worth less over time (that is, it purchases less). Instead, you need to plan on putting money to work for you through investments that increase in value so that you earn enough to maintain your life style in face of rising prices.

Tax Risk

Tax risks arise when government policy favors or punishes certain forms of income. The uncertainty of tax consequences complicates investment decisions, and tax risk also shows up when you plan to sell something and find that the tax consequences are significant.

For example, you have been in your home for a year and a half and lose your job. The house has appreciated in value quite a bit, so you plan to sell it and move to a new location where jobs are more plentiful. However, since you have lived in the house less than the time specified in the tax laws (currently two of the last five years), you will have to pay tax on any profit you make on the sale of the house. If you can postpone moving and selling your home until you have lived in the house for the two years, you may not owe any tax. (This example harkens to a time when housing prices were rising rather than collapsing [before 2008], but the tax example remains valid.)

Tax laws are extensive, highly complex, and always changing. Tax consequences impact every decision you make about savings and investing. Get professional tax advice any time you are making major money decisions.

Legal Risk

An investment's attractiveness is affected by the degree to which various statutes and regulations may impact the business. Real estate, for example, is subject to an enormous array of zoning and building laws. More than one promising development never got further than the drawing board because the project became uneconomical when restrictions were imposed on it. Be extremely cautious of assuming a positive outcome in highly regulated situations. "Is this legal?" is always a worthwhile question to ask.

The Risk of Job Loss

Changes to the workplace are constant. Your willingness to accept investment risk is modified by your job stability. Be certain that your cash is not tied up in such a way that you cannot access it should your job situation change. It is reasonable to have the equivalent of six months' to a year's pay in highly liquid, low-risk investment instruments. Bank accounts are a good choice.

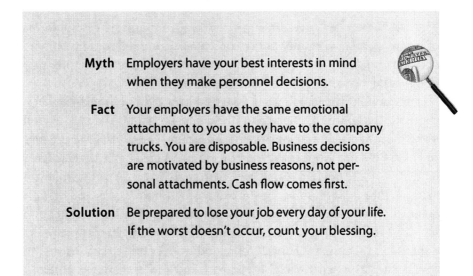

Myth   Employers have your best interests in mind when they make personnel decisions.

Fact   Your employers have the same emotional attachment to you as they have to the company trucks. You are disposable. Business decisions are motivated by business reasons, not personal attachments. Cash flow comes first.

Solution   Be prepared to lose your job every day of your life. If the worst doesn't occur, count your blessing.

The Risk of Ignorance

Failure to understand the wide array of risks can cost you money. Do your homework in advance so that you are never in the position of saying, "If I had only known that, I would not have . . ."

Summary

Insulating yourself totally from risk is impossible. Avoiding one risk automatically brings into play an alternative risk. Balancing risks is a constant challenge.

Six points are worth remembering as you enter the world of investing:

1. **Know yourself.** Do not journey beyond your level of competence. Continue to learn and seek professional advice. Read. Take your time.

2. **Diversify.** "Do not keep all of your eggs in one basket" is nowhere more applicable than in money matters.

3. **Buy only what you understand.** Merchants of investment products are forever creating exotic and complex schemes for beating the odds. Some are legitimate. But if you do not thoroughly understand what you are getting into, better to be safe than sorry. Avoid the latest, greatest, cannot-fail, guaranteed sure-thing fad. Billions upon billions of dollars in recent losses by the biggest, most well-known, prestigious giants of the investment banking universe are evidence enough that no one has a crystal ball for the future. Avoid the herd instinct.

4. **Ask "How do you get paid?"** It is impossible to obtain unbiased advice from someone whose income is tied to that advice. For example, life insurance chartered life underwriters (CLUs) are very well trained, but make no mistake, their bias will be toward life insurance products because they make their living from commissions on sales of life insurance products. This bias is perfectly ethical, but nonetheless you must take it into account when you are trying to plan your future.

5. **Do your homework.** Information is everywhere and very accessible. There is no excuse for not learning what you need to know; if you're in the dark, it's by choice. The time spent learning about investing will minimize bad decisions and reduce stress in your financial life. There is no one right answer, only intelligent choices.

6. **Pay for professional advice.** At some time you are going to be faced with financial decisions that have major consequences, are irreversible, and are beyond your own level of expertise. Find a "fee-only" financial advisor who does not sell any products. The advisor's modest fee will be more than balanced out by the costly mistakes his or her advice will prevent you from making.

CHAPTER TWELVE

Government Programs

No book on personal finance and money management would be complete without comments on the role of government in your financial life.

In the space of one chapter, it is impossible to do anything more than sensitize you to the fact that nearly every financial decision you make has some government twist to it. In no other aspect of financial decision making is it more important to do your homework and seek the services of a paid professional than in government regulation. Many financial decisions you will make are irrevocable, and ignorance of the law will not protect you from the consequences of the law. Proceed with caution!

Why There Are Government Programs

Governments at all levels are engaged in three primary activities:

- **Raising revenue to run the government (taxing):** Income taxes, property taxes, and sales taxes are the major sources of revenue for governments.

- **Controlling people and their activities:** Laws, including tax laws, are passed to encourage or discourage certain behaviors deemed socially necessary, desirable, or undesirable. Traffic laws, building codes, zoning laws, licensing laws, and consumer protection laws are just a few of the controls imposed by government.

- **Social engineering—changing things to fit politicians' policies and biases:** Combining revenue activities and control activities is growing as politicians feel it is within their legitimate roles to rearrange things more to their liking.

The Federal Tax Code

The Internal Revenue Code has by far the greatest impact on financial planning. The code itself is a massive and largely unintelligible document that is further complicated by rules and regulations administered by an administrative army. Changes and amendments occur continuously, so what was true or correct yesterday may be incorrect or even illegal tomorrow. This complexity makes long-range planning difficult and perilous.

It is legal and it makes common sense to use the tax laws for your personal benefit. It is foolish and costly to ignore the advantages the tax code may provide to you.

Encouraged Activities

Savings

The government's encouragement of long-term savings is the area of government-sponsored activity most likely to impact every person. The U.S. government recognizes that people should take responsibility for their own futures and has enacted a wide variety of laws to encourage savings.

Common to all of the programs is some variation of both the timing and the amount of taxes in exchange for restrictions on accessing the money. An underlying but unstated assumption is that money saved (or invested) will grow and be worth more in the future. Recessionary economic cycles may prove this assumption wrong, but for all practical purposes it is the accepted assumption for planning the future.

401(k)s

The 401(k) is one of the best known long-term tax-deferred programs. The 401(k) works like this: You are allowed (actually encouraged) to have your employer deduct up to 10 percent of your earnings from your pay before taxes. You do not pay current income tax on the amount of your income that you have saved in the 401(k) plan. This program limits the amount that can be deducted from your paycheck each year, and that maximum changes from year to year and increases after you reach age 50. The earnings in 401(k) accounts also accumulate tax free.

When you start taking money out of your 401(k) (no sooner than at age 59½), the withdrawals are then taxed. It is assumed that when the average person starts taking money out of the 401(k), he or she will most likely be in a tax bracket that is lower than the bracket during his or her working years. The idea is to end up with more money than you would have had if you had taken post-tax money from your paycheck and invested it.

Employers have been moving away from the defined-benefits retirement programs that historically were based on your time with the company and your earnings. Instead they are focusing on defined-contribution-type plans such as the 401(k). A vast majority of employers have a "matching" program for such plans. Typically, for every $1.00 you put into your 401(k) from your pay, the employer puts in another $0.50 up to a certain maximum, say 6 percent of your pay.

A 401(k) with employer matching is the absolutely positively best deal on the planet. You earn an immediate 50 percent (the $0.50 matching) on your money! The very first priority in your money management plan is to take advantage of any 401(k) plan up to the maximum matched by your employer. Even while you are working your way out of debt, this step also needs priority.

Individual Retirement Accounts (IRAs)

If your employer does not offer a 401(k) plan, you are probably eligible to open an IRA with pretax dollars. Not everyone is eligible for an IRA, so you need to check with a financial expert. The traditional IRA is funded with money on which the government allows you to pay no taxes currently (pretax dollars). When you withdraw funds from the IRA, you are then taxed for the amount withdrawn, including accumulated earnings.

A Roth IRA has different eligibility requirements and is funded with after-tax dollars—those on which you have already paid income taxes. The Roth withdrawals, including the accumulated earnings, are tax free.

Other Tax-Favored Programs

Many other tax-favored plans exist for a wide variety of situations. Programs to set aside money for college tuition and medical savings accounts are two worth mentioning. If you have children headed for college, you owe it to yourself to investigate options that will make paying for tuition easier.

Money set aside in tax-favored accounts is highly restricted as to when and how you can withdraw it and may be subject to severe penalties if you ignore the rules. My best advice is to seek professional guidance when setting up these programs. A little caution can save you major problems.

Home Ownership

Owning a home is another government-favored activity. Interest paid on your mortgage is deductible for income-tax calculations, as is your local property tax (that is, mortgage interest and property taxes may lower the income tax you owe). The idea is to make owning a home more affordable.

If relocation is in your life plan and you have to sell your home, it pays to make sure you get the tax advantages by getting professional help. For example, should your home have appreciated in value, you may escape a large portion of the gain being taxed when the home is sold. Currently, if you have lived in your home for two of the past five years, a gain of up to $250,000 is tax free. The amount is $500,000 for a couple.

Unfortunately, if your home has lost value, as many people are now finding to be the case, there is no deduction for your loss.

Leaving your home to someone else when you die has some real tax advantages if you do it right and some real perils if you do it wrong. Consult a professional.

Stepped-up Basis

"Basis" is accounting jargon for the amount you have invested in an asset. It is usually your cost. Basis is used to determine the gain or loss on which tax will be assessed.

For example, you buy 100 shares of BigCo for $50 a share, or $5,000. Later you sell the stock for $100 a share (or $10,000). Deduct the basis of the stock from the sales price to calculate gain ($10,000 sales price – $5,000 basis = $5,000 gain). You made a $5,000 gain, which is taxable income.

If you give the shares to someone, that person assumes your basis and pays tax on the gain when he or she ultimately sells the shares. However, if you instead leave the stock to the person in your will, the tax code currently gives the person a "stepped-up basis" to the market value as of the date of death. The same is true of the transfer of other assets.

Let's see how this might work. Joe invested in a sure thing and bought 10,000 shares of FabulousCo for $1.00 apiece; he then promptly forgot about it. Thirty years have now gone by, and Joe is planning his affairs and doing his will. He still has the 10,000 shares, which have appreciated nicely, and they are worth $25.00 each. In hindsight, it really was a sure thing.

If Joe sells the shares, he will owe tax on the difference between the $1.00 (his cost basis) and the $25.00 they are now worth. That will be tax on $240,000! If instead he leaves the stock to his son, his son's basis will be $25.00 per share—the value of the stock at the date of his father's death. The son can sell the stock and owe no tax on the entire $250,000. If he holds the stock and it ultimately becomes worth $30.00 a share, his tax on sale will be on the $5.00 gain.

Again, the rules are intricate and perilous. Get professional help.

Investing

Government tax policy is mixed on investing and is likely to change. Gains on investment that are realized in less than a year are known as short-term gains, and they are taxed at the same rate as your income tax rate. If the gain is realized after a year, it is known as long-term gain and is taxed at a significantly lower rate.

Dividends and interest also get preferential tax treatment through lower tax rates, but as with other investments, the particulars of that treatment are likely to change.

Discouraged Activities

While it is legal to minimize your taxes, the government frowns on avoiding taxes with questionable schemes. Tax shelters, as they are popularly known, are complex efforts to manipulate the tax laws. Many are legal, many are not. If you are in the earnings bracket to be considering tax shelters, you are certainly able to afford the very best professional advice. Be sure to get it.

Timing

On the one hand, most tax-deferred programs (IRAs, 401(k)s, and CDs) have severe penalties for withdrawing the money before certain prescribed times. Age 59½ is typically the earliest (with some strict exceptions) that you can take money out of a retirement account without penalty.

On the other hand, the government does not want you to avoid paying taxes forever and has therefore imposed mandatory distribution beginning at age 70½.

Other Policy Areas

Government laws discourage bankruptcy, short-term investments, and accumulating large amounts of money (estate taxes and gift taxes). Large accumulations of money are, at a person's death, subject to estate tax, and during one's life, the government restricts one's gift giving through gift taxes.

Other Government Help

In addition to managing our lives largely through tax laws and regulations, governments also invest a substantial amount of money in financial and consumer education programs. Many of these can easily be found through an Internet search. Whenever you are searching for information, be sure to take advantage of government programs and materials.

Strategy for Dealing with Governmental Impact

When dealing with the impact of government in the world of your money, my advice is consistent: Read and read some more to immerse yourself in the money world so it will bit by bit become less intimidating and you can avoid big blunders.

However, I must also emphasize that you should seek professional help on *anything* that involves significant amounts of cash or securities or that involves the transfer of assets from one form to another or from one person to another. A certified public accountant (CPA), an attorney, or a fee-only financial planner can save you many times their modest fees.

The intricacies and interactions of laws are beyond most people's ability to master. Popular guides should only alert you to the fact that there is more to learn than you can handle. Doing it yourself is not recommended for legal issues.

Summary

Sometimes the government is really there to help you, and at other times it will go to great lengths to stop you from doing certain things. Sometimes you can't figure out who is on which side. Continually expanding your own understanding of your financial life is a must.

CHAPTER THIRTEEN

Insurance

Insurance is a risk-protection product for disasters that are likely to occur but the details of when and where are unknown. The concept of insurance is a relatively late innovation of modern civilization that has its roots in fire insurance for homes and cargo insurance for ships.

Fire insurance is a specific example of the function of insurance. In a community of, say, 500 houses, the probability that one of them will catch fire each year is predictable. What is not certain is which house will catch fire. If each homeowner shares the cost of repairing the one that catches fire, no one suffers the whole catastrophe. The money paid into the pool of funds to cover the loss is the insurance premium. (In reality, fewer than one in 500 houses catch fire.)

Ship-cargo insurance is another early form of insurance, and its workings are fascinating. When a ship is loaded with cargo, all of the shippers want their cargo to be delivered safely to the buyer at the end of the voyage. Insurance underwriters are skilled in assessing the risks of transit and will issue an insurance policy guaranteeing the value of the cargo. If the ship sinks, the insurance pays.

But what happens if the ship gets in trouble, part of the cargo is tossed overboard to save the ship, and ultimately the ship arrives with only some of the cargo intact? Who pays? Marine cargo insurance policies have a provision known as the general average clause. It states that the ship's owner and each of the cargo owners are assessed "pro rata" for the loss of the jettisoned cargo. All the other shippers benefited and because the whole ship was not lost, all should pay for that benefit. So even though one cargo owner's goods arrived intact, his insurance company would pay a portion of the loss of the cargo that was jettisoned to allow his cargo to survive the voyage.

From the humble beginnings of ship and fire insurance has sprung the complex modern insurance industry. What you need to know is the different kinds of insurance that should be a part of your life.

First-Party Insurance

The kind of insurance that protects you from the loss of your own property is referred to as first-party coverage. The automobile collision coverage and comprehensive coverage in your automobile policy are everyday examples. If your car is smashed up by you or anybody else, the insurance company pays for the loss. Homeowners' fire insurance is another example. If your house burns, the insurance company pays.

Insurance is economically profitable to private commercial companies only when risks are spread among large numbers of insured, most of whom are unlikely to need the insurance (for example, private companies insure cars because only a few people are likely to have an accident).

The terms of first-party policies describe exactly which hazards are protected against and which are excluded. Flood insurance is not covered on homeowners' policies because the only people who would opt to buy it are people who are really likely to get washed away—people who live on the seashore or along the banks of a river, for instance. The U.S. government sells flood insurance instead of private companies. In California, an earthquake-prone state, private companies do not sell earthquake insurance for the same reason.

Insurance rarely pays 100 percent of a loss. Deductible amounts are paid by the policyholder before the insurance pays. Without deductibles, premiums would be too high to afford.

To save significant amounts of the cost of both automobile and homeowners' insurance, increase your deductibles. Ask your insurance agent how much various deductibles would save you; by raising your deductibles, in a few years you will save enough on your insurance premiums to establish that emergency fund you've been hoping to build.

Third-Party Insurance

Insurance that you buy to protect you from liability for damage, injury, or harm that you cause another is third-party coverage. The property damage and personal injury portions of your automobile policy are examples. If an accident occurs and the insurance carrier determines you are at fault, the insurance carrier will attempt to settle the claim. If your insurance company thinks you are not at fault, the company may refuse to pay. If you get sued, the insurance company will defend you.

An umbrella policy is another type of third-party coverage. It is a personal protection policy that covers you from liability for things not covered either by your homeowners' policy or by your automobile policy. Umbrella policies are very inexpensive and worth buying.

Life Insurance

The purpose of life insurance is to provide money for your beneficiaries to replace the money you would have provided to them had you not inconveniently died. Life insurance comes in many forms.

The most basic form of life insurance (and the cheapest) is the term policy. A term life insurance policy is for a specific term; for example, 5 or 10 years. The premiums increase as you get older, and at some age you will probably not be able to buy term insurance at all. Term life is the least expensive way to get large amounts of coverage when you are younger and in good health and when you have dependents who would be severely impacted by your untimely demise. Term life insurance has no cash value accumulating.

Permanent life insurance (sometimes referred to as "whole life") is a product that combines insurance and investment. Your premium is established at the time you buy the policy and never changes. Dollar for dollar, permanent life insurance costs more than term insurance but has the advantage of building up cash value over time (so it is also an investment).

Within the life insurance family are endless variations of policies well beyond the scope of this book. Start out with term insurance to protect your family and then learn about the other choices.

Health Insurance

Health insurance has become an important part of everyday life. Because the concept of health insurance is shifting from paying only for major health care needs like surgery to covering all of a person's health care, costs have escalated. Costs will continue to rise dramatically and will become a critical part of future planning.

The shift is actually away from the original concept of health insurance as an instrument that spreads the costs of low-frequency events over many policyholders to insurance under which everyone expects coverage for "maintenance" items. That costs are higher is hardly surprising. It is not unlike having your homeowners' policy pay for annual carpet cleaning. The more coverage that is going to be offered, the higher the costs will be. There is no spreading of the risk, which is the underlying concept of insurance.

One of the issues facing the health insurance industry is the concept of "insurability." Historically a person has had to be in good health at the time a policy was written to qualify for the insurance. Under political pressure, health insurance is coming to be viewed as a right—irrespective of whether a person is in good health or not.

The laws surrounding health insurance are changing rapidly, and you need to keep up to speed on the choices available, the relative costs, and the benefits to you. The complexity and broad scope call for a whole book on this subject alone.

Income Protection

If you are disabled and cannot work, you need some way to pay the bills. If you are hurt on the job, workers' compensation pays some income replacement, but the amount is very low and inadequate for most people.

Short-term income continuation insurance may be available through your employer for a reasonable cost or may be included in your regular employment arrangements.

Long-term disability policies cover your lost wages for certain periods of time when you cannot work at all or when you cannot work at your regular job. The cost of the policy is related to how soon the policy starts after the beginning of a disability and how long a period the policy covers. Some of these policies may be available through your employer and are worth investigating.

Miscellaneous Insurance

Insurance is available to cover almost every conceivable situation. A few of the types available include:

- Trip cancellation insurance
- Accidental death and dismemberment insurance
- Travel insurance
- Long-term care insurance
- Warranty extension insurance
- Home repair insurance
- Mortgage payoff insurance
- Credit card payment insurance in the event of job loss

When buying any insurance, it pays to shop and bargain. Decide how much risk you can afford to accept yourself. Are you willing to cover the first $1,000 damage to your car in the case of an accident (a $1,000 deductible) or would you be more comfortable being responsible for only the first $250? The choice (and the resultant price for the policy) is yours.

Insurance Investment Products

Whereas the original concept of insurance was simply to spread risks among a large group so that no one person would suffer catastrophic loss, insurance companies have evolved into selling investment products.

Critics of life insurance as an investment instrument contend that if you buy the cheaper term insurance and invest the difference in the premium costs, you will have better long-term investment results than the insurance investment offers. This is open to debate and depends on many assumptions to either prove or disprove one's opinion.

Insurance agents have many arguments in favor of whole-life policies; an unstated one is that their commissions are much much higher on whole life.

The vast majority of financial planners advocate buying term life insurance for the protection you need separate from your investment goals.

Annuities are another well-known insurance investment product. Money is paid into an annuity to set it up, and distributions are made from the annuity. These are extremely complex products, and no one should invest in an annuity without professional guidance from someone other than the person selling the annuity.

Summary

Insurance is an essential component of any financial system and needs to be applied on an individual basis. One size definitely does not fit all.

The more you study and learn, the better equipped you will be to make sensible insurance-buying decisions.

CHAPTER FOURTEEN

Credit Scores and Identity Theft

The topics of credit scores and identity theft are being covered together because they are inexorably intertwined. Become a victim of identity theft and one of the first consequences will be a change to your credit score.

History of Personal Credit

Once upon a time, as noted earlier, when you needed to borrow money, you began by filling out a multipart application form. This form followed a tortuous trail through the credit approval process, in which actual people scrutinized the form. Their analyses were aimed at discovering (1) whether you had the ability to repay the loan and (2) whether your history showed a willingness to repay the loan. In short, were you creditworthy?

Unfortunately, the process was as much an art form as it was analysis, and it was fraught with personal biases. Things that had little or nothing to do with creditworthiness crept into the decision process, including your age, race, religion, sex, marital status, address, and other personal details.

Fast-forward to the twenty-first century, and we have largely replaced the old system with objective, fast, and fair analysis-based credit scores. Bias or discrimination is virtually impossible, so more people qualify for credit than was possible under the old system of individual underwriting. Credit scores are derived from your past responsible or irresponsible use of credit. The assumption is that you will be consistent with that past pattern, whether good or bad, in the future.

Your FICO Score

FICO, the best known and most widely used scoring system, was developed by the Fair Isaac Company and is named after that company.

Five areas of your financial life are factored into your FICO score, with the following relative levels of importance:

Payment history	35 percent
Amounts owed	30 percent
Length of credit history	15 percent
New credit	10 percent
Types of credit in use	10 percent

For a really simple and comprehensive explanation of credit scoring and identity theft, go to www.myfico.com/crediteducation/brochures.aspx. There you will find two reports:

- Understanding Your FICO® Score

- Identity Theft and You

Do yourself a big favor—download these reports right now and study them carefully. What you learn will dovetail nicely with your newfound personal financial management expertise. Avoid future surprises by learning what you should be doing now.

Get Your Credit Reports

Information for your credit score originates primarily from periodic reports companies make to one or all of the three credit bureaus (TransUnion, Experian, and Equifax). Other information is derived from public records, such as bankruptcy filings. Obviously, if the information the credit bureaus receive is incorrect, your record will be wrong. Therefore it is incumbent upon you to monitor every credit report regularly to spot errors and get them corrected.

You are allowed by law to receive a free credit report every year from each credit bureau. Plan to order one report every four months from a different credit bureau and review the report carefully. By rotating among the bureaus you will have a current report three times a year. Then start the process over each year. You should obtain credit reports frequently enough to detect any problems, and remember that one of these reports annually from each bureau is free. By requesting copies of your credit report regularly, you can detect identity theft, which I will cover in more detail in the following pages.

The site for your free credit report is: https://www.annualcreditreport. com. Several companies offer to get your credit reports for you and to provide assorted other services for a fee. They may or not be worthwhile for you, but remember you can get reports free.

The credit bureaus do not give you your FICO score, but you may want to obtain that score separately. There may be a fee. The site for FICO is: http://www.fico.com.

If you are turned down for credit, you are entitled to know which credit bureau provided the lender information that was used for the decision, and you are entitled to a free credit report at that time as well.

If there are errors on your report, the procedure for correcting or disputing them is clearly spelled out for you.

Know Your Rights

Go to http://www.ckfraud.org to download a listing that summarizes your rights under the Fair Credit Reporting Act and a listing of the addresses and telephone numbers for the three credit bureaus. Below are the numbers for requesting a credit report. Other numbers are available for reporting fraud, for opting out of preapproved offers, and for disputing information on your report.

The three credit bureaus are:

- Experian, 888-397-3742

- TransUnion, 800-916-8800

- Equifax, 800-685-1111

While the electronic age has brought many blessings, it has also introduced some negative aspects. Each of us is now a digital number instead of a person, and that makes it easier for someone to impersonate you (to steal your identity) if you are not extremely cautious about your privacy.

Identity Theft

It is time to become paranoid. There are people out there who want to steal your good credit and use it for themselves. It is easier to steal your identity than it is to break into your house and steal your possessions, which may or may not appeal to the burglar's tastes. By stealing your identity, thieves can select precisely the make and model of the product they want and charge the purchase to your account!

You lock the door to your house when you go out. You lock your car when you park. You must learn ways to protect your identity from being stolen.

Identity theft can take many forms. At its simplest, thieves merely use your credit information to make purchases. Ultimately the charges show up on your bill, and you have to challenge them.

More complicated "application fraud" (or name fraud) occurs when a thief steals your name and Social Security number and opens new accounts in your name. It may take you a long time to find out about this type of fraud because the bills will be mailed to the imposter's address. Losses can be enormous, and the time to repair your reputation can be very long indeed.

The following material is excerpted and adapted from the Federal Trade Commission pamphlet *Avoid ID Theft: Fighting Back Against Identity Theft,* available from www.ftc.gov/idtheft.

Common Ways Thieves Steal Your Information

The common ways identity thieves steal your personal information include:

- **Dumpster diving**. They rummage through the trash to find personal information.

- **Skimming**. They steal credit/debit card numbers when processing your card.

- **Phishing.** They pretend to be your bank or some other company to get you to reveal your personal information.

- **Changing your address.** They change the address on your billing statement to their own address.

- **"Old-fashioned" stealing.** They steal your purse or wallet or mail.

How to *Deter* Thieves

Here are some key ways you can deter identity thieves by safeguarding your information:

- Shred documents before they go into the trash.
- Protect your Social Security number.
- Don't give out personal information on the telephone.
- Never click on links sent in unsolicited e-mail.
- Don't use an obvious password.
- Keep your personal information in a secure place at home.

How to *Detect* Suspicious Activity

You should routinely monitor your financial accounts and billing statements in order to detect suspicious activity. Signs that require immediate attention include:

- Bills that do not arrive as expected.
- Unexpected credit card or account statements.
- Denials of credit for no apparent reason.
- Calls or letters about purchases you did not make.
- Discrepancies that you pinpoint when you inspect your credit reports (as explained above), review your billing statements for accuracy, and compare charge receipts to the statements.

How to *Defend* Against Identity Theft Losses

As soon as you suspect identity theft, here's how to minimize your exposure:

- Place a fraud alert on your credit reports.
- Close accounts that have been tampered with.
- File a police report.
- Report the incident to the Federal Trade Commission.

You are responsible for your own security. Take this very seriously by following the previously discussed deter, detect, and defend guidelines. Maintaining security is a continuous process of daily vigilance. Don't become an inadvertent victim and in hindsight wish you had been more diligent.

Privacy Rights Clearinghouse

Another "must visit" resource has been introduced earlier in this book. The Privacy Rights Clearinghouse is an outstanding organization whose mission is looking out for you. Three of its reports are particularly on target, and you should download them and study them carefully. These free reports may be obtained at www.privacyrights.org.:

- **Fact Sheet 1:** Reducing the Risk of Identity Theft.

- **Fact Sheet 17(a):** Identity Theft, Victims Guide: What to Do If It Happens to You.

- **Fact Sheet 23:** Online Shopping Tips

Elder Fraud

Closely related to identity theft is the whole area of elder fraud. It is sad to report that the occurrences of preying on senior citizens are increasing. Criminals understand just how vulnerable the elderly may be, and they have no qualms about stealing from them in ever more sophisticated ways.

Summary

You work hard for what you have. Protect your creditworthiness and actively guard against identity theft. Several years ago a resident in a small Southern California town whose house had just burned to the ground was being interviewed on the local TV evening news. The reporter asked if the owner had fire insurance on his home. The owner replied that he did not have insurance. "Why not?" the reporter asked. "Because," the homeowner replied, "I have never needed it before!" Don't wait until you are a victim to protect your identity. You need to do it now.

CHAPTER FIFTEEN

Emergency Preparedness

Are You Ready?

You may have tackled the issue of preparation for an emergency, but for the vast majority of people, being able to meet the specter of a disruptive emergency is not a high priority. It should be.

More articles and tip booklets than you could read in a month have been written about what you should do now to prepare for a "What if . . ." scenario. If you live in a flood area, tornado zone, hurricane path, or earthquake zone, you are more likely to have some plan in place because a natural disaster is likely. For example, residents in areas where heavy snow is common have emergency supplies set aside because they realize they should plan to be snowed in for days on end. Also, if you live in an area subject to regular natural disasters, you may have made some preparations because local regulations mandate some measures. For example, in Florida building codes mandate window shutters, and in California new structures are required to be built to withstand earthquake shaking.

All of these situations are sufficiently predictable and recurring to motivate people to be ready for them . . . theoretically. But what actually happens? And what about preparing for less likely but equally devastating events? How will you cope when your routine is instantaneously disrupted?

Natural Disasters

At 4:31 AM, January 17, 1994, the Northridge earthquake occurred in California. Minutes later my cul-de-sac was teaming with men, women, and children who had just fled their houses from the violent shaking. It was pitch black. Although many had elaborate evacuation plans, not a single family had followed their plan. No one had a grab bag of essentials. No one had a clue as to how to find out if anyone was missing or trapped inside. A few had flashlights. No one appeared injured. No fires had broken out. Calm prevailed, but it was overlaid with confusion.

It was a week before we had water, electricity, or telephone service. Although ours was an equestrian community, no one had stored water for the horses. Teenagers bailed water from swimming pools into barrels and went around the neighborhood watering the horses.

In the weeks that followed, everyone changed their attitudes about being prepared for the next earthquake.

Systems Overload

In Washington, D.C., two deranged snipers were killing people randomly. Stories by TV and radio commentators had created a frenzy of fear and confusion. Within a very short time, the number of cell phone calls increased so dramatically that the system was overwhelmed. Nobody could get calls completed, which made the problem even worse.

Can these examples happen again and to you? Of course they can, but it is more likely that something unexpected will happen and you will have to react—like the bridge collapsing in Minneapolis or a truck filled with toxic chlorine gas turning over on the freeway near a residential street.

Preparation

Preparation begins with your own mental attitude and acceptance of the facts that (1) sometime there can and will be a disaster that affects you and (2) you have to be prepared to look out for yourself.

Disasters come in many forms: A widespread catastrophe is vastly different from a more localized one, and, as was clearly demonstrated during Hurricane Katrina, external resources may be overwhelmed. In planning, counting on others to rescue you is naïve.

An event that to some people is a full-blown disaster may be viewed by others as a mere inconvenience. The difference is in experience and planning. Better planning usually translates into less risk and less financial loss.

A good plan factors in all of the variables that can make things worse.

Duration

One variable of any disaster is duration. Is the situation short term (like a snowstorm) or is it permanent? Weather-related events, while of maximum inconvenience, pass relatively quickly. A nuclear meltdown like Three Mile Island or Chernobyl lingers forever and requires different coping strategies.

Area

The Northridge earthquake, as violent and costly as it was, covered a relatively small geographic area. Support facilities and massive resources were nearby and available immediately. At the other end of the spectrum, Hurricane Katrina covered a vast geographic area. In the short term, the resources to address a loss of such magnitude simply were not readily available. Help was a long time coming and was a long distance away.

Weather

Any weather extremes compound problems. In the Northridge quake, there was no danger of freezing to death in Southern California in January. A disaster at the same time in North Dakota would be compounded by the subfreezing temperatures.

Magnitude

Not only is the area affected relevant for planning, but also the intensity of the event must be taken into account. A tornado is violent and anything in its path is doomed. A hurricane can do marginal damage, or it can be strong enough to level a large city, as Hurricane Andrew did in southern Florida. Small earthquakes rattle people as much as they rattle the dishes. Big earthquakes do big damage but usually in a small area.

When preparing your plans, you need to address each of the preceding variables. For some of them you will simply accept the risk that they are improbable and do nothing. During the Cold War, many people built underground shelters for protection against nuclear attack. Others figured the possibility was remote and skipped preparation. Only you can decide what is right for your circumstances.

Creating an Emergency Plan: Three Time Frames

Three separate time frames should be addressed in planning: immediate short-term emergencies; medium-term emergencies; and long-term emergencies.

Immediate Short-Term Emergency (72 hours to 1 week)

Try this exercise. Go outside right now and stand about 50 feet from your house. Assume you cannot go back inside and are being told to evacuate your property. Your car is in the garage and you cannot get it out. What do you need to get through the next 72 hours alone? What other assumptions do you make? In the worst case, there is nobody nearby to help you.

The preceding scenario is a good starting place for making a short-term emergency supply list. Think like a solo backpacker heading for a week in the mountains.

Medium-Term Emergency (1 week to 6 months)

The resources you need to make it for 6 months are much different from the previous timeline.

Assume your place of employment suffers a fire and you are going to be out of work for six months. What do you need? It is obvious that this contingency requires a broader plan than simply having a "grab-and-go" kit sitting in the garage or in the trunk of your car.

Long-Term Emergency (over 6 months)

Anything that totally disrupts your life for over 6 months falls into the category of a long-term emergency. The situation may be job related (you change jobs or suddenly retire), health related, or relationship related. The unexpected death of a spouse who is the principal wage earner is an example. Divorce, loss of job, accidents, and natural disasters all have the potential to be in this category.

Emergency planning encompasses much more than just the immediate. It must address the rest of your life. Admittedly, events like retirement are not technically "emergencies," but the planning process is the same.

A Comprehensive Plan

A comprehensive plan that addresses all three types of emergencies is the best way to minimize the personal and financial impact of emergencies.

The plan must cover at least these areas for each time frame:

- Food and water

- Health and safety

- Shelter

- Communication

- Transportation

- Money/cash

- Documents

- Clothing

- Tools and supplies

- Assets and possessions

Table 15.1 provides an example of a way to organize your planning. You need a plan for every box on the table. A few examples are discussed below. Do you have a plan for each of these areas with which everybody in the family is familiar?

Planning Example: Money and Cash

Although this chapter doesn't have enough space to cover all of the preceding planning areas, let's examine one area, money and cash, as an example to give you an idea of what's needed. For short-term emergencies, you must assume that credit cards may not work, banks will be off line, and ATM machines will not be operating. Merchants may insist on cash. You should have from $100 to $300 in small bills set aside somewhere likely to be accessible if you have to leave your house, but concealed so the money is safe.

Table 15.1   Emergency Planning Checklist

Planning Area	Scope of Emergency		
	Short-term: 72 hours to 1 week	Medium-term: Up to 6 months	Long-term: Over 6 months
Food & water			
Health & safety			
Shelter			
Communication			
Transportation			
Money/cash			
Documents			
Clothing			
Tools & supplies			
Assets & possessions			

Reminder: Full-size forms may be downloaded from our Web site: www.ptff.net

A medium-term emergency is anything not in the budget that occurs when you are not expecting it or haven't planned for it. An automobile accident is an example. A job loss is another. To cover medium-term emergencies, prudence suggests you have at least six months' net pay in highly liquid investments such as money market accounts or short-term certificates of deposit.

And finally, you need enough money to last through retirement. These funds will probably be a combination of savings, investments, and retirement accounts including Social Security. (For more detail on just how much money you will need in retirement to replace your paycheck, refer to Chapter 10.)

Another Example: Assets and Possessions

Assets and possessions are another emergency planning area. For short-term protection, you may have fire extinguishers, locked storage, or a safe deposit box. For medium- and long-term protection, insurance policies provide a safety net.

More Information

Two Web site resources for emergency-planning details, particularly on short-term emergencies, are:

- http://www.ready.gov/america/publications/allpubs.html
- http://www.fema.gov/areyouready

Summary

Financial planning is not just about cash and what's happening this week. It is a state of mind that helps you anticipate unforeseen events and be prepared for them. Once again—it is up to you.

CHAPTER SIXTEEN

The Secrets of Making Lots of Money

If you are like most people, you have occasionally wondered why someone makes lots of money. Also you wonder whether you could someday be one of those making the big bucks.

Nearly all highly paid jobs and massive incomes like those earned by celebrities in sports entertainment can be explained by two variables.

1. They do very well something that is difficult to do.

2. What they do has economic value to someone else.

Both are always present when someone is highly paid.

Difficult to Do

What does "difficult to do" mean? This quality should not be confused with "hard to do." Physical exertion required is not a measure of difficulty. Plenty of jobs are "hard work" when measured by physical effort required. Restaurant servers, construction workers, truck drivers, auto mechanics, and hair stylists, just to name a few, all do very *hard* physical work and are tired when the day is over.

In our context, "difficulty" is related to how many people can do a job or can learn to do it in a reasonable time period. The more people who can master a job, the easier we can conclude the job is. The fewer people who can (or do) learn to do it, the more difficult we can conclude it is. For many fields of employment, jobs can be classified along a continuum. Bookkeeping is relatively easy to learn. Becoming a certified public accountant is harder to learn. Becoming a corporate tax accountant is tougher still. The harder what you do is to learn (determined by how many people achieve the skill), the higher the wage you can expect to earn.

A nurse undergoes quite a bit of training and is well paid. A doctor undergoes even more training and is more highly paid. A neurosurgeon is a rare person indeed, requiring both extensive training and a great deal of talent. Therefore it is not unexpected that a neurosurgeon's pay is much higher than a nurse's pay. What the neurosurgeon does is more difficult.

Some jobs demand that they be filled by only the best in the field. In such cases, requiring extraordinary talent is also considered to make a job difficult. Jobs in professional sports and the performing arts thus are considered difficult.

Economic Value

Difficulty is only one dimension of making lots of money. The second dimension is "economic value." The task that is difficult must have economic value to someone else who is willing to pay for the skill. Engraving the Gettysburg Address on a grain of rice is certainly difficult to do. It is unlikely that there are many people who can do this. What is even more rare would be finding someone who is willing to pay for the grain of rice bearing the Gettysburg Address.

The astronomical salaries paid to entertainment celebrities and sports stars are examples of economic value. Not all football quarterbacks play well enough to lead their teams to the Super Bowl or even to the playoffs. The quarterbacks who play at this level are not just paid because they do a difficult job well. Rather, such players are highly paid because they do something difficult well *and* their play/persona has a direct economic benefit to the owner. The owner knows that the fans love heroes and superstars and will pay to attend games at the stadium to see them play.

Singers who sell lots of records, actors who make successful movies (as measured at the box office), and super athletes who fill the arenas are all making more money for someone else than they are being paid. As soon as their economic value goes away, so does their high pay.

Everyday Jobs

In the world of more mundane work, the two factors of difficulty and economic value also hold true.

For example, salespeople are among the highest paid jobs in every industry. Why? Because selling is difficult! And because of the nature of selling, it is easy for an employer to measure the economic value of a person's skills. A successful salesperson may earn a very high income if—and only if—there is positive measurable sales performance.

Of course, income for jobs in sales is often unreliable. Successful sales may equal high pay, but poor sales likely equal lower income. Many people do not want this risk factor in their pay, so they willingly take lower-paying nonsales jobs that have predictable income.

What to Do

How can you personally benefit from these observations about the highly paid?

Scarcity is an indicator of "difficult to do." Scarcity, or the reality of supply and demand, can help guide you toward a more financially rewarding career. Identify those areas where "doers" are scarce yet in demand. See if you can become one. You will need diligence and willingness to invest time to learn something new, and for some occupations some talent may be required.

Sometimes doers of a certain job are in short supply because the job is distasteful or dangerous. Are you willing to do things others shy away from? If so, your openmindedness may be your ticket to a higher-paying job.

The Exceptions

As we all know, the world is not always fair. Keep in mind that doing something difficult of value to others does not *guarantee* you a highly paid job, and not all who hold such jobs obtained the positions on merit alone. Some people get the high-paying jobs because of their connections and who they know. This phenomenon is particularly common in the closed cultures of large corporations. But your odds are better if you know the underlying rationale for high income.

Invest in Yourself

Give Yourself a RAISE focuses on teaching you how to improve your financial life by getting the most mileage possible from the dollars you are now earning. Another step you can take to better your financial life is to invest in yourself to become more valuable to your employer. Chapter 17 has some tips on how to do that.

CHAPTER SEVENTEEN

Five Secrets of Success

Pat Bleil, Ph.D.

Publisher's Note: *Pat Bleil is the Chair of the School of Management Studies at Eastern University, Director of the MBA program, and Professor of Management. She teaches communication skills, leadership, marketing, ethics, research design, and statistics. In addition she has researched and is known for her work in mentoring women in executive management.*

Prior to joining the university, she was Vice President of Sales of a Fortune 100 company where she supervised a sales force of over 600 people generating in excess of $1 billion in sales. In this capacity, she has recruited, trained, supervised, and disciplined a veritable army of individuals. This is her chapter, and her advice is both sound and based on practical experience and will help lead you to a successful career.

One: First Define Success

How do *you* define success? Success, like beauty, is in the eye of the beholder. The first step in being successful is to write out your very own definition of success. The statement should be clear enough that you can measure yourself against whatever scale you want. What will success look like once you achieve it? In other words, what is your vision?

An example of a good vision statement is the one President John F. Kennedy made about going to the moon. It went something like this: "We will put a man on the moon by the end of the decade and return him safely to Earth." It did not specify how we were going to do that, but it was absolutely clear how we would measure success or failure. Either we got there, or we didn't. No place for vagueness there!

Nothing is more demoralizing than trying to meet someone else's expectation for you. Success is personal, and nobody can achieve it for you, no matter how well intended they are. Parents take note. Encourage your kids to strive for their own success, counsel them, guide them, and introduce them to the world's reality, but don't tell them how you will measure if they are successful or not.

Your definition of success will change over time. That is okay. Set your sights far enough in the future and high enough that there is challenge in reaching success. But do not set your goals so far in the future or so lofty that the probability of actually being successful is remote or impossible. You need to enjoy incremental success.

Thomas Edison was said to have been asked if he became discouraged when his 25,000 different attempts to invent an electric light bulb had failed. He philosophically replied that he was not discouraged because he now knew 25,000 things that wouldn't work. Most of us cannot survive those long odds.

Early in this book, you began the task of reaching financial success, and that included setting goals. Goals organize your life and provide guidance for your activities. Success depends in large part on setting priorities and then resisting distraction by activities or expenses that do not lead you to success. If you find yourself straying from your goals, take a fresh look at them. Are they truly your goals or should they be revised?

A lawyer once boasted to a number of his associates that he had never lost a single case. His colleagues were well aware that a number of criminals whom he had defended were guests of the state in the penitentiary, and they confronted him with this seemingly contradictory fact. "Yes," he admitted, "but I have always gotten paid."

Success, it seems, depends on how you choose to keep score. Step one is therefore to write your very own definition of success.

Two: Take Charge of Your Life

Just as your definition of success is personal, it is up to you to take the steps toward success. Life is full of choices. Within reason we can do almost anything to which we aspire, but it is unrealistic to think we can do everything we want to do. Nobody can succeed for you. Accept responsibility for yourself. Have a plan and follow it, or revise it. Be content with what you have, not sad about what you do not have.

Three: Invest in Yourself

Successful people are always growing. They embrace change and take steps to make change work for them. Time and money you invest in self-development pay off better than almost any other investment, not only in monetary rewards but in the personal satisfaction derived from growing.

You cannot rest on your past achievements. You have to keep growing. I once had a poster that said simply: "Nothing You Have Done in the Past Will Ever Again Be Good Enough."

Three kinds of personal growth have strong relevance to job opportunities.

Technical Skills

The world of technology is changing faster all the time. The ways things were done just a few years ago are now obsolete. Just keeping up with innovation in your own field of work will help assure that you will be in demand in the future.

Communication Skills

Dealing with others successfully is an ability that is in high demand. When working to get results through others, you need either power or persuasion. Persuaders do better over time than those who rely on power to get results. The art of listening deserves practice. The art of asking questions is a cornerstone of good communication skills.

Decision-Making Skills

Every day we face a wide variety of decisions, from the very simple (such as what to wear today) to the incredibly complex. Sorting them out is always challenging, and the worst sin is procrastination or doing nothing. The ability to make the "right decision" is a valuable skill, and that is defined as making the decision that is appropriate to the situation at hand. This skill is called judgment.

The process of problem analysis is in demand in the work world and in your personal life. Books on negotiating skills, salesmanship, and problem solving are plentiful and worth your time.

Among the best self-development books ever written is Steven R. Covey's *The 7 Habits of Highly Effective People.* One of the most powerful quotations in Covey's fine book is: "The successful person has the habit of doing the things failures don't like to do. They don't like doing them either necessarily. But their disliking is subordinated to the strength of their purpose."

Four: Get Help

You are not alone. The abundance of resources is mind boggling. For anything you want to learn or any skill you want to develop, books, classes, and personal help are readily available. There are no barriers to knowledge other than your own inertia or failure to reach out for them.

Five: Don't Be a Pain in the A _ _!

The sad truth is that many highly competent and well-qualified employees are passed over for promotion or more responsibility simply because they are hard to get along with. The single most powerful driving force in every decision anyone makes is comfort. Given an array of choices on anything, the decision-maker always favors the choice that is most comfortable (or least stressful or uncomfortable). Comfortable mediocrity always wins out over stressful excellence.

We avoid people we do not like.

If you can be excellent in what you do and a pleasure to be around, you have increased your chances of promotion a thousandfold.

Conclusion

Give Yourself a RAISE right now. You have the tools and direction to do it. Plug the leaks in your spending habits to get more discretionary money.

Get out of debt and stop paying interest that buys you nothing and instead increases the price you pay for everything charged. Live within your means. Invest in your future so you can command higher pay. And finally, be content with the blessings you have.

Just do it.

About the Author

Gordon Bennett Bleil is renowned for his ability to present complicated material in such a fashion that it becomes simple and understandable.

In *Give Yourself a RAISE*, Bleil demystifies personal money management for those struggling to gain control of their finances.

Having an MBA in finance and drawing on his practical background as an adjunct professor of management, successful business owner, and bank executive, he is able to distill good money management to its understandable fundamentals.

Over his career, Bleil has taught in MBA programs at a number of institutions including John F. Kennedy University and spent many years as an executive in and consultant to the banking industry. Most recently he hosted the radio talk show *The Path to Financial Freedom* and has taught training courses of the same title to employees of various businesses—including the Cancer Treatment Centers of America.

Unique to this book are three features Bleil created to help individuals manage their finances:

- A Financial Freedom Risk Assessment Quiz to evaluate your risk of losing your financial freedom

- The Freedom Money Management System™ to take advantage of the incredible power of electronic banking in organizing your personal finances

- A simple and comprehensive goal-setting system to begin your journey to financial health and simultaneously eliminate family money conflicts

Financial troubles cause untold misery to countless individuals. Bleil is dedicated to helping those in financial distress find their way out of trouble and reach a permanently stable financial footing.

CPSIA information can be obtained at www.ICGtesting.com
Printed in the USA
LVOW05s1554110114

369055LV00018B/946/P